EMOTIONAL INTELLIGENCE 2.0

I0425554

IMPROVE YOUR SOCIAL SKILLS &
BUSINESS RELATIONSHIP BY
INCREASING SELF CONFIDENCE.
BOOST YOUR EQ THANKS TO
POSITIVE PSYCHOLOGY COACHING &
SELF DISCIPLINE (FOCUS ON
MINDSET)

by **Stephen Joseph Maxwell**

Congratulation on purchase this book and thank You for doing so.

Please enjoy !

© Copyright 2019 by

Stephen Joseph Maxwell

Table of Contents

CHAPTER 1...1

EMOTIONAL INTELLIGENCE.............................1

UNDERSTANDING EMOTIONAL

INTELLIGENCE...19

    Here are six tips to increase your emotional

    intelligence:...29

CHAPTER 2...31

    THE FIVE MAIN COMPONENTS OF

    EMOTIONAL INTELLIGENCE............................31

    SELF-AWARENESS...34

    SELF-REGULATION...48

    INTERNAL MOTIVATION....................................55

        Best Modes of Internal Motivation...................62

        Crying Helps...63

        Exercise and Your Hormones............................65

    EMPATHY..67

    SOCIAL SKILLS..81

CHAPTER 3...96

    THE CHECKLIST TO FIND OUT IF YOU'RE

    EMOTIONALLY INTELLIGENT..........................96

CHAPTER 4...117

    FAILSAFE STEPS TO DEVELOP SOLID SELF-

    AWARENESS..117

    REMOVE...122

REFLECT...126

REACT...128

RESPOND 130

REPEAT...133

CHAPTER 5...136

EFFECTIVE TIPS TO HELP YOU UNDERSTAND

OTHERS..136

KNOW THE PRODUCT.......................................138

KNOW THE INDUSTRY......................................139

BE PERSONABLE..140

GIVE THINGS AWAY 142

GO THAT EXTRA MILE 143

USE THE RIGHT LANGUAGE............,...............144

OLD SCHOOL IS BEST SCHOOL......................146

HUMAN SCHEDULES...147

NLP...148

TIPS FOR READING PEOPLE'S THOUGHTS.149

THE POWER OF COMMUNICATION 150

WHAT CAN WE LEARN FROM THE NEAR

DEATH EXPERIENCE?.......................................152

GOOD RELATIONSHIPS 154

CHAPTER 6...156

LEADERSHIP AND THE SECRETS OF

MOTIVATION 156

CHAPTER 7...170

CRUCIAL IDEAS WHICH HELPS TO AVOID

SOCIALLY AWKWARD SITUATIONS............170

BODY LANGUAGE 172

HUMOR 174

TALKING TOO MUCH OR TOO LITTLE........175

LYING 176

DEFENSIVENESS...177

WAYS TO AVOID AWKWARD MOMENTS

WHEN MEETING SOMEONE NEW 178

KEEP IT LIGHT 179

SHARING TOO MUCH INFORMATION........181

DO NOT COME ON TOO STRONG.................183

USE YOUR SOCIAL GRACES............................185

HAVE AN EXIT STRATEGY 187

Tips on Treating Social Anxiety Effectively .188

CHAPTER 8...193

IMPROVE RELATIONSHIP WITH EMOTIONAL

INTELLIGENCE 193

Reflection questions for a difficult conversation:

....195

1. Self-awareness: 201

2. Emotional maturity:.....................................202

3. Self-motivation: 202

4. Empathic understanding:...........................203

5. Quality communication:.............................204

EMPATHY ON RELATIONSHIP 205

1. Slow down and still your mind.................206

2. Listen and Pay Attention............................207

3. Feel and Let go..208

4. Express yourself 209

5. Accept unconditionally 210

HOW TO USE EQ IN DIFFICULT

CONVERSATIONS? 212

1. Clarify your own purpose and intent. 212

2. Build a foundation for the conversation ...214

3. Stay focused on jointly designed process .216

4. Agree to monitor progress and discuss again

....217

STRESS MANAGEMENT 219

EMOTION MANAGEMENT...............................221

CHAPTER 9..**223**

ENHANCE EMPATHY 223

STAGES OF EMPATHY 229

THEORY AND THERAPY....................................234

CHAPTER 10..**246**

DOES YOUR BRAND HAVE EMOTIONAL

INTELLIGENCE? 246

CHAPTER 1

<u>EMOTIONAL INTELLIGENCE</u>

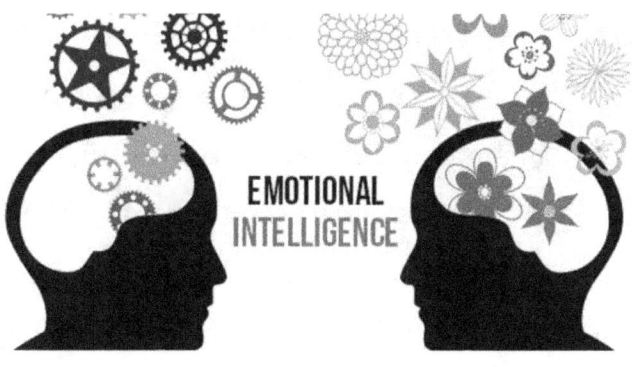

Emotional intelligence is probably not a phrase you hear too much. it is still a fairly new field and many experts are still not in agreement as to what this type of intelligence truly measures.

However, its popularity as a study of human personality is growing all the time. in the sphere of human intelligence there are two very distinct areas; that of cognition and intelligence. however, the area of emotional intelligence does not fall within either cognition or intelligence.

Studies have been conducted as to how and how quickly a person can change between one emotional state to another. of course, this is not an exact science. there are many differing parameters and variations depending on the person being studied and the circumstances involved. we all act differently to different situations, the emotional response will never be a constant. these variables are of course the major problem in determining how to accurately measure emotional intelligence.

There is no clear dividing line between intelligence and knowledge. some state that emotional intelligence totally dynamic, can be increased and decreased, will change with each person and with what that person is experiencing. yet others claim the total opposite stating that people's emotions are constant and therefore are not affected by any situation. my personal opinion is that i tend to disagree with the latter.

Despite these conflicts there seems to be one constant belief, that our emotions are something that are developed over time. in other words we are not born with our emotions and develop them as we grow and learn. we can therefore say that emotional intelligence is our capacity as human beings to define our own emotions by the people, the circumstances and events we encounter, our environment.

We use our emotions to control how we react to situations and is therefore a major factor in determining our personality, who we are. the number of definitions as to what emotional intelligence really is are, of course, far too many and complex for this short article however, what we can confirm is that there are two constants in all this. firstly, the concept of what emotions are and secondly, understanding the context of emotions.

Emotions are far more than simply how we feel about something or someone, they are what drive us to be and do. They can energize and motivate or even immobilize us.

How often have you heard "I work better under pressure", maybe you have even said it yourself. When we are in love we can do more, be more, talk into the wee hours of the morning without becoming tired... and without wanting the conversation to end.

The truth of the matter is that without emotional energy we would be far more passive. It is emotion that helps us study for the degree we want, put in those late nights or last minute spurts to complete a presentation. Emotion inspires us to take the leap and ask a woman out, and helps us to stay awake through the night nursing a sick child.

Unfortunately emotion is also what stops us from achieving our goals, freezing us up in fear, keeping us awake at night as we worry about things we said or didn't say, unpaid bills and work performance.

Think of it this way, the reason we wake up in the morning may be because our bodies have had enough sleep but why exactly do we get out of bed? The answer is anticipation of events which provides the stimulus to keep us engaged in this world. This may be slight oversimplification, ignoring so some more complex biological factors but think about it, think about how waking up in the morning you begin thinking about the day ahead.

What you anticipate may be positive or negative, but the biological response is principally the same, it causes the sympathetic nervous system to kick in, truly waking us up and getting us ready for action.

But let's look at this, nothing has actually happened... you are simply anticipating what may happen and experiencing thoughts around this. And it is not only in the early morning before the day has started that our thoughts influence and govern our emotional response to stimuli. As a result these thoughts are where your power exists, the power to influence not only your emotional response but your energy and drive to live life to its fullest, to achieve your dreams and exceed your expectations.

The challenge to recognise your "emotional thoughts" and train yourself to develop thoughts which energize and motivate, thoughts which create a sense of self reliance, where your emotions are not at the mercy of others, or events which are beyond your control.

Emotional intelligence involves a set of skills that help us to perceive, understand and influence our own and others feelings. Workplaces that either don't have these skills, or don't encourage people to apply them, aren't fun places to work. Beyond this, they're also highly unlikely to be as effective or productive in the long term, as the people in the business never truly connect and collaborate with each other. For long term success, businesses need leaders that inspire people, connecting the hearts and minds of all employees. These businesses need emotionally intelligent leaders.

Leaders high in emotional intelligence are connected to the people around them. They present as authentic and empathetic, willing to practice expansive thinking, constantly seeking to include and understand rather than exclude and ignore. This means resilient and empowering leadership that isn't afraid of others opinions and doesn't feel the urge to have the final decision or always be proved correct. These leaders are centred and in control of both themselves and the world around them, which inspires confidence and trust, creating an atmosphere where employees energetically collaborate to produce the best possible results for the business.

The question is - who do we think of when we reflect on our own personal experiences of emotionally intelligent leadership? The sad truth is that, for most of us at least, there's a relative paucity of these people in the places we work. The majority of businesses still think of emotions and feelings as valueless and reward people not for HOW they get results but WHAT results they deliver. As a result, when we consider our own experiences, we are far more likely to recall distracted and busy leaders that don't have time to listen or who don't really listen even when they're sitting in front of us watching our mouths move.

The good news is emotionally intelligent leaders are 'out there' somewhere; and some companies are even actively seeking to foster and encourage these people. These businesses aren't blazing a trail of innovation and cutting edge practice. They're simply accepting that there is a better way of doing things. They believe that creating a better place to work is achievable, and that assessing and developing the necessary skills is far from rocket science - it's actually tried and tested practice that has been around for years.

Emotionally intelligent leaders understand how events and triggers in the workplace result in emotional responses. They come to terms with the fact that these emotional responses are based on prejudices that have formed through a combination of their experiences, beliefs and values. They are aware of how this cocktail of perceptions and the loose recollection of facts influences them, the behaviours that can result (if this influence goes unchecked), and what these behaviours and emotions can mean for the people they work with.

The outcome of this knowledge is that they are aware of the impact their feelings and emotions have upon their thought processes, which allows them to minimise the times when this can inhibit their effectiveness at work. This strengthens their decision making immeasurably. By becoming aware of their own emotions and how they manifest, they also become more connected with their employees.

Take, for example, the experience we've all had of the manager who becomes inflamed by the messenger whilst failing to address the content of the message. We've all had to impart bad news at some time or another - and it just doesn't help if we know that the recipient is likely turn a shade of red or jump to conclusions. Emotionally intelligent leaders understand what events trigger strong emotions and they're aware of when it happens. This allows them to express these feelings appropriately, better manage the situation constructively, and - most importantly of all - avoid negatively impacting on the employee that brought them the problem in the first place.

By understanding their own feelings emotionally intelligent leaders become better equipped to express themselves. This skill allows them to help others understand and engage with their decision making, whilst also becoming more authentic with the people they work with. This enhanced understanding and authenticity improves their interpersonal connections right across the business, which significantly increases their interpersonal effectiveness.

This improved emotional expression builds trust and mutual understanding with their colleagues - from which greater collaboration and cooperation springs. Rather than being perceived as 'vulnerable' for expressing themselves, these leaders win hearts and minds with appropriate levels of honesty. The key here is that they learn to express themselves in the right way, to the right degree, at the right time, and with the right people.

The benefits to a business of a leader who can appropriately express themselves are twofold. Firstly, there are no surprises and people know where they stand with these individuals. This dramatically reduces 'avoidant' behaviours and encourages open dialogue. Secondly, their honesty allows everyone in the business to better understand and interpret the decisions they make. This will engage employees more with these decisions, as well as increasing the likelihood that they'll fully and properly ensure their execution.

By combining what they know with how they (and others) feel, emotionally intelligent leaders can make better decisions by being more expansive and inclusive in their approach. This allows them to build more effective teams, playing to the strengths of individuals, whilst also understanding the limitations and 'blind spots' of each employee. This, in turn, results in more energised cooperation and collaboration, which 'gets things done' and fosters greater innovation.

These leaders see emotions and feelings as vitally important, not to be overlooked, and usually predicated on important subconscious thoughts, experiences and knowledge. By tapping into the emotional and feeling aspect of each employee they can help people keep open minds, explore and reiterate ideas as they flow around the business, and expose employees to situations that will bring out the best in them.

Ever wonder why there isn't much collaboration or cooperation in some businesses? The answer is likely to be found in the way the leaders, and employees who mirror their behaviours, manage facts and feelings. Facts will be treated with a premium - the currency with which knowledge and status is acquired. Feelings, on the other hand, get in the way of making fact based decisions: they add no value and muddy the water.

The problem with this approach is that everyone has feelings. Managing facts and not managing feelings has only one inevitable conclusion: a business where people don't care about or understand one another. It's no wonder then that the people working in these businesses don't collaborate or cooperate. They're far too busy dealing with facts to care about the people sitting next to them.

Being self aware and aware of the feelings of others, and then expressing and reasoning with these feeling, is only the beginning. Once emotionally intelligent leaders are aware of how they (and others) feel, and the consequence of these feelings, they set out to actively manage and control them in a way that produces dramatically improved results for the business.

This active management and control makes them resilient rather than emotional and empowering rather than indifferent to their employees. Their observable behaviour makes them appear more centred and in control - a calming influence on those around them. These emotions and behaviours are contagious: with positivity breeding positivity. They develop this proactive control and management through reactive emotional management techniques (such as breathing control) and proactive emotional management techniques (such as working to change their mindset from negative to positive with regard to specific situations).

UNDERSTANDING EMOTIONAL INTELLIGENCE

We are all familiar with general intelligence (IQ). How many of us know anything about Emotional intelligence (EQ)? Emotional intelligence is the capacity to identify, apply, empathize and manage emotions in positive ways to communicate effectively, understand others, fight challenges, relieve stress and resolve conflict in an intelligent manner.

Daniel Jay Goleman an eminent author, psychologist, and science journalist wrote a book on Emotional Intelligence in 1995 which turned out be an internationally best-selling book. Ever since then it has become a buzz word in the fields of psychology and sociology. Soft skill modules and trainers are reiterating on the importance of emotional intelligence in work place and in social settings.

In order to gain success and happiness in life, emotional intelligence is needed as much as intellectual ability (IQ). Emotional intelligence is helpful at work, in relationships, in career growth and personal goals. From here on we will refer to Emotional Intelligence as EQ.

How do you boost your EQ? You could increase your EQ by learning and mastering a few key skills:

First of all it is important for you to understand the fact that your emotions impact various aspects of your daily life - the way you carry yourself, the way you behave and the way you interact with others. With a high EQ you are capable of recognizing your own emotional state and that of the others. This understanding helps you to communicate and convince others in a way that draws them closer to you. The success with which you are able to use your EQ leads to success in every path of your life leading to more contentment in life.

There are four main qualities or characteristics of Emotional Intelligence: "Knowing yourself is the beginning of all wisdom" said Aristotle. This wisdom holds the key to further develop your EQ.

Self-awareness: Did you ever stop to think who you really are inside? Whether you are good or bad, clever or dull, witty or serious, etc.? Well, when you sit in a place and observe yourself as an outsider you may be able to understand the real 'you'. When you look at yourself deeply you may understand why you acted in certain ways under certain circumstances. The ability to introspect yourself is self-awareness. Self-awareness helps you identify your thoughts, actions, feelings, values, fears, shortcomings, strengths and overall the total 'you'. Besides yourself you can approach your loved ones and friends to make you understand you. You can get a feedback from those who will give you their honest opinion of you. This helps to a certain extent how others perceive you. In marketing this is done through a questionnaire about a company's product and performance. This is evaluated and used in improving the company's products and services. In the same way you could ask your loved ones to evaluate you and from their answers you could understand and improve your EQ in areas where you lack. As an adult you could do this exercise in form of a journal. In fact journaling is a great way to see the real you and your genuine feelings. You are more in tune with your own feelings when you have a high EQ. this in turn increases your self confidence in life, in dealing with yourself as well as others.

Self-management: Self-awareness leads to self-management. Self-management is all about controlling your emotions and actions. You control yourself from impulsive behaviors. You develop openness, adaptability, achievement and optimism. How do you react to certain situations? Do you respond or react to people and situations? It is a slight difference between these two words but in practice there is a great difference in meaning. Reaction and response play a significant role in EQ. For example if you have to wait in long line on a busy day when the traffic is moving ever so slowly, do you get impatient? Do you scream at other drivers and horn loudly or wait patiently for the traffic to clear? Do you react or respond to heavy traffic? If you are impatient you are reacting to traffic in an emotional way.When you react you tend to lose reason. On the other hand if you show patience you are responding and therefore more understanding and thoughtful. After all, the traffic has to move on at some point! Self-management stands for adaptability, transparency, achievement and optimism.

Social awareness: Your self-awareness and self-management takes you to the next step of social awareness. You are open to understanding the needs, emotions and concerns of other people. You are able to pick up on emotional cues, feel relaxed socially, and recognize the power play in a group or organization. In order to develop your EQ you need to see and feel others in their shoes. People with excellent social awareness are said to be more service minded, have empathy and organizational awareness. These are the main traits associated with social awareness according to Daniel Goleman. Social awareness at its best is offering a natural response to people, taking their situation and needs into account as much as possible. If you exhibit these qualities you can consider your EQ to be high.

Relationship management: The final area you need to develop in raising your EQ is that of relationship management. We can look upon this trait in connection with your profession. This is the aspect of your EQ that enables you to succeed in inspiring other people and helping them to reach their full potential. It is also vital in negotiating successfully, resolving conflicts and working with others toward a shared goal. Your success in this final area is directly correlated to your success in the other three areas because management is all about successfully interacting with other people. At the end of the day isn't efficient management all about getting the work done?

Goleman stresses on the following aspects for a successful relationship management:

- <u>Leadership</u> - develop others by identifying their strengths; Influence others probably through your own motivation

- <u>Communication</u> - being a change catalyst to incorporate new ideas when change is needed
- <u>Conflict management</u> - connecting with people through networking
- <u>Teamwork and collaboration -</u> by giving credit to everyone to make them feel good about their own contribution.

How does Emotional intelligence affect your life?

Performance at work - EQ helps you to comfortably handle social complexities of workplace, motivate and guide others and succeed in your career. Now-a-days companies view emotional intelligence as being an important aspect and perform EQ testing before hiring.

Physical well-being - Stress is imminent in today's world no matter which profession you belong to. Stress is a familiar factor leading to serious health issues in most of the people. Uncontrolled stress level is known to increase the risk of heart disease. Our immune system suffers when stress level are high.

Mental well-being - Stress affects mental health negatively. You might have read or heard about stressed people going to the extent of committing suicide. When you cannot manage your emotions you become a victim of mood swings or other mental disorders that can seldom allow you to form or maintain strong relationships in life.

Personal relationships - Understanding your emotions help you to express your feelings to your loved ones. When there is a block in communication your relationships suffer both at work and in your personal life.

Here are six tips to increase your emotional intelligence:

- Learn to reduce negative emotions

- Stay cool and manage stress
- Be assertive and express difficult emotions when necessary
- Stay proactive, not reactive in difficult situations
- Bounce back from adversity
- Express intimate emotions in close, personal relationships

If you prefer you may write these in 6 different tips and post them in places where you can see to incorporate them in your daily life.

Emotional Intelligence (EQ) is an art to be developed in these times in order to intelligently tackle your emotions in every situation in life. This ability paves way for success and self satisfaction in every sphere of your life.

CHAPTER 2

<u>THE FIVE MAIN COMPONENTS</u>
<u>OF EMOTIONAL INTELLIGENCE</u>

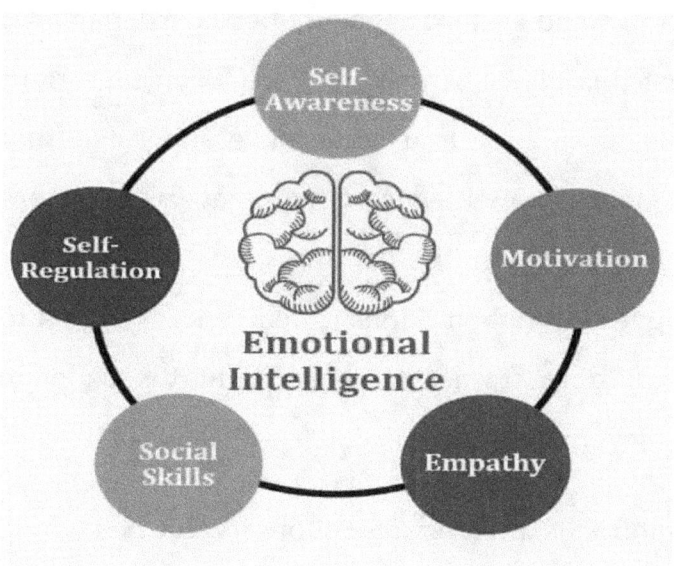

Have you ever known people who always seem to keep their cool, who are able to handle even the most awkward social situations with grace, and who always seem to make others feel at ease? Chances are pretty high that those individuals possess what psychologists refer to as emotional intelligence.

Emotional intelligence involves the ability to understand and manage emotions. Experts agree that this type of intelligence plays an important role in success, and some have suggested that emotional intelligence might even be more important than IQ. In any case, research has suggested that emotional intelligence is linked to everything from decision-making to academic achievement.

Emotion is a wide range of observable behaviors, expressed feelings, and changes in the state of mind and body. Feelings, emotions, our likes, and dislikes, give our individual lives meaning and cause us to be happy or unhappy, satisfied or dissatisfied. Intelligence is the ability to acquire and apply knowledge and skills.

Emotional Intelligence is the ability to deal with other people successfully.

The following includes a brief overview of the 5 main components of Emotional Intelligence. The main identifying characteristics of Emotional Maturity are made possible by the Emotional Intelligence component.

SELF-AWARENESS

Emotional intelligence starts with emotional self-awareness. Self-awareness requires accepting emotional experiences as real, valid, legitimate aspects of human experience and instead of denying emotional responses or reactions to situations, using the emotional information to make better decisions and take actions. Emotional self-awareness allows an individual to feel better or to do things better depending on the actions he or she takes in response to emotions, as opposed to reacting merely to soothe or stifle unpleasant and intense emotional sensations.

Consider your own experience of converting fear into competence. Every child is told to avoid a hot stove, and on occasion an overly-curious child burns his fingers on the stove-only to learn a very painful lesson. However, most of us do not cower in fear whenever we walk into a kitchen. We recognize that the fear of being burned turns into a well-informed caution and a respect for the power of flame. As a result of our own experience, and recognizing our emotional response, we process fear and turn it into the ability to perform a task: we respond with caution to an open flame rather than react out of fear to the possibility that we might get burned.

While emotions are subtle and combine in complex ways, it is useful to model emotions on a simple "palate" from which more complex emotions are construed. The spectrum of emotions follows the pattern:

Anger - Sadness - Fear - Happiness

That is, this model suggests that anger is closer in modality to sadness than fear; fear is closer to sadness than anger; and happiness is closer to fear than sadness.

To understand your emotional response to an event, think of a goal you highly prize. It could be seeking a promotion; it could be recognition for a job well done; it could be the success of your firm. Make sure it's an important goal to you.

Now imagine someone outside threatens your goal, using an unfair tactic. A coworker misrepresents a situation and costs you a promotion. A competitor sends in senior managers to steal one of your key accounts. In this situation, you most likely feel anger directed toward the other person because they intentionally and somewhat maliciously did something to block your goal. In general, anger is directed toward an agent, another person or group, who actively blocks our goal.

Compare this to the feeling you would have when that same goal is not available, but there is no one to blame. Maybe the promotion vanished because of a downturn in the economy. Maybe your key account simply has no need for your services anymore. Since there is no agent that actively blocked your goal, your goal is now simply lost. Most likely you feel sadness at the loss, since your goal is not attainable but it is not anyone's fault (not even your own).

Suppose now your goal is in an unknown state. Maybe it's threatened by another person, or maybe you're waiting for news as to whether the customer will continue to use your services. In that uncertain situation in which you are waiting for resolution you most likely experience fear of your goal being lost, which will later settle into sadness or anger when you become certain of the outcome. Fear involves having your goal in an uncertain, possibly positive and possibly negative, state.

Finally, assume you get surprise news that your goal has been met. Your promotion has been agreed upon by your managing partners and will be granted three months early. Or your key account has decided to double their projected work with you because of an upturn in the economy. With your goal unexpectedly facilitated and achieved, you most likely feel happiness given the unexpected result. Happiness occurs when a goal we have worked toward is achieved, and the sudden or surprising nature of the news can create excitement; just as sudden news can create anxiety that leads to sadness in the negative case.

This exercise provides insight into how your emotions inform you about your circumstances and can guide your response. If you are angry, for example, the questions you ask yourself include: Who are you angry with? What goal did he or she block? To resolve the situation, can the offender to modify his or her behavior? Do you reorient your goals?

This level of self-awareness will make emotions more valuable, even integral to your decision making. Emotions are not to be avoided, but rather embraced as essential tools to allow managers to make better decisions.

Your self-awareness resides in your brain. Your sense of self goes wherever your brain goes. But what if we duplicate your brain thingy? There appears to be two ways of doing that: the technologically-assisted 'natural' way (cloning), and the technological way (downloading).

There's no theoretical reason why a human being, such as you, could not be cloned. The only reasons against doing that in the here and now are ethical and legal reasons. However, the brain of a cloned you would be a blank slate, since all those nebulous traits like memory and morality could not be cloned. But what about the self-awareness part of the brain? Presumably your most faintest stirrings of self-awareness begin at conception and increase as the complexity of your entity increases. Presumably a clone of your brain, all things being equal, would have the same chemistry and neural connections. But, all things probably aren't going to be equal. There will probably be external and environmental influences which will alter, even if just subtly, the brain chemistry (diet, drugs, etc.) and neural pathways (disease, injuries, etc.) of the clone. Therefore, I suspect that your clone would not have your self-awareness and vice-versa. Your clone is in the exact same category as your identical twin.

The other, yet to be achievable, technological methodology of duplicating your self-awareness would be to download it into another form of hardware - not squishy wetware biology but as bits and bytes software into some sort of suitable receptacle, call it a computer if you will, perhaps with artificial arms and legs attached - a robot/android. [A cyborg would result if your actual squishy brain thingy were placed in an artificial receptacle or container or constructed body.] Again, there will have to be lots of legal and moral issues sorted out first, but the technology to do this should be achievable. So, the awareness of self in your biological squishiness will be the same as your awareness of self as, say a robot. Now the interesting thing is that you, your self-awareness, could be downloaded hundreds of times over, just like you can copy and paste a document on your PC. How could you cope being self-aware hundreds of times over in hundreds of different places? This might be akin to a hive-mind or to a computer network.

Which then leads to the next stage: if one could create a self-aware artificial intelligence (AI) then that could be copied again and again, then presumably whatever one AI entity experienced, all would experience. And with that we really enter the realm of science fiction.

Fly in the ointment #1: If there is a biological entity (human or animal) in one place that is a self-aware entity; and there is another biological entity (human or animal) in another place that has the exact same brain chemistry and neural network structure, then the latter entity presumably has the same self-awareness as the former. For each to be not only self-aware as being their own entity but self-aware as being the other entity too, wouldn't there have to be some sort of telepathic exchange (call it communication if you will) between the two separate and apart bodies? How would that work? Actually it doesn't logically follow. If you self-aware in another body there's no need for communication of that fact since you are already self-aware of it.

Fly in the ointment #2: The most likely answer to this whole one self-awareness per customer issue might like in the statistical improbability of it all. Yes, very unlikely things can happen. It's not inconceivable to toss a coin heads up 1000 times in a row; a monkey pecking away at a typewriter could reproduce say the U.S. Constitution. It just might be the case that the number of combinations of brain chemistry and neural network connections is just so vast, that the number of possible combinations, the number of possible self-aware entities, exceeds by many, many orders of magnitude the numbers of actual self-aware entities that have and every will likely exist. Therefore, the possibility of two or more entities sharing an exact state of self-awareness is just about the same as a tornado tearing through a junkyard and assembling a replica of the White House.

An Extra Chain of Thought:

Some, especial spiritual and New Age types suggest that the cosmos is and always has been self-aware or has consciousness because the cosmos contains entities that are self-aware (like us). We (for example) are the universe's way of contemplating its own navel - of knowing itself. But I think several problems arise with that point of view.

Firstly, there was a time the universe contained no self-aware beings, even microbes. The spiritual types however extend self-awareness down to self-aware rocks and atoms and even electrons that have awareness of self. That's an interesting but deluded worldview IMHO.

Secondly, if we accept that rocks and atoms and even electrons do not have awareness of self, we note that the cosmos is mainly composed of just that sort of non-aware stuff, from the macroscopic (stars and rocks, etc.) to the microscopic (atoms and electrons). That rock in your garden isn't self-aware even if you, your pet dog and your garden plants are. In other words, can a cosmos be said to be self-aware if only the most minuscule part of that cosmos is aware of itself?

Thirdly, a self-aware universe (as defined by having self-aware inhabitants) would have to have an overall self-awareness that was a composite of all the self-aware entities in it which would also change and evolve as self-aware entities came into being, evolved, and then died out. What sort of self-awareness would result if you merged into one great melting pot all of the individual self-aware entities currently in existence on Planet Earth? It would be a dog's breakfast methinks.

SELF-REGULATION

Controlling your impulses — instead of being quick to react rashly, you can reign in your emotions and think before responding. You express yourself appropriately.

Failure to self-regulate is central to all current world problems. Addictions, abuse, violence, war, crime, under-achievement, debt, and obesity are all at epidemic proportions. In contrast, no negative patterns are associated with personal self-control. Self-regulation functions like a muscle where initial fatigue results in greater strength, and repeated exercise over time develops greater control. It is unclear as to whether self-regulation can be taught; scenarios and conditional statements may help. Is it the nature of the child or the nurturing of the parent that is most responsible for self-regulation? We can demonstrate the process, but ultimately it is the will of the individual that determines replication, practice, and behavior change.

Continuous improvement is a concept and process that allows us to move on an upward spiral of growth and renewal. Professor Edward Deming validated this process when he was commissioned to help rebuild Japan in post-war construction. He taught top management personnel that they could increase productivity and expand their market share by improving the quality of their products. They applied his process and the results are revealed in the high quality of items produced in Japan today. Like the manufacturing process, we can also refine ourselves as we apply his process to gaining greater self-control.

The four steps of the Deming Cycle are: PLAN, DO, STUDY, ACT.

PLAN- As with any positive goal, an operationally defined statement of what is to be accomplished must be established. This is the "TO BE" statement. To quote a familiar adage: "If you don't know where you're going any road will get you there" (Lewis Carroll, 1832-1898). The present "AS IS" condition is a declaration of fact that acts as a baseline from which to show improvement and growth. For example, people wanting to adjust their weight would start with an awareness of their current weight before they could take action to change it. Periodic measurements would determine whether you are losing weight, gaining weight or remaining stable. The "AS IS" condition must be assessed and described prior to beginning work towards the "TO BE" vision. An accurate assessment of the past must occur which leads to the present in order to identify variables that ought to be considered. Weaknesses discovered become the basis for a personal plan of improvement.

Finally, personal reflection is highly recommended as this process progresses.

DO- This is the performance step of the cycle. This involves implementation to the best of your understanding and ability the actions that were planned previously. Monitoring behavior under a variety of conditions or environments is essential. Notes should be taken to monitor significant behaviors and insights against the "TO BE" vision.

STUDY- This is the evaluation step of the cycle. It is an actual review of where you are after your recent effort, against where you are trying "TO BE." Critical assessment of the process or behavior is required. The observations of the DO step are used to determine what will best measure change. Discovering the "why's" behind the undesirable behavior is critical. These insights and data are invaluable for the next step.

ACT- Analyze the insights identified in the previous step. This involves taking these identified behaviors that are resulting in less-than-desired outcomes, and adjusting them to the "TO BE" vision. Each insight will be part of one or more PLAN,DO,STUDY,ACT (PDSA) rotations. Determine where to apply changes to continue improvement. Once identified, they must be incorporated into your daily routine to begin witnessing improvement. Comparison of where you were at the "AS IS" stage against where you now are determines the degree of improvement.

The spirit of continuous improvement compels you to begin the cycle again, repeating the steps as before: **PLAN, DO, STUDY, ACT**. Each cycle results in refinement, improvement, and mastery with regard to the defined target of self-control. As with any new skill, practice makes perfect. In time, self-control will be noticeably improved, refined, and modified. In time you will be thinking, acting, and behaving at the next higher level. It is critical to establish an "AS IS" statement, which becomes the benchmark for improvement. Self-reports, at best, are biased and are subject to extreme respondent prejudice and so, working with a trusted friend or mentor will ensure greater accuracy in results. As with any continuous improvement process, change is the driver.

INTERNAL MOTIVATION

Motivation is something that should be internal. You can do a lot to change the environment around you, so that you are surrounded exclusively by positively motivating forces; however, you will never able to separate yourself from all of the negative influences. For this reason, it is critical that you develop a strong sense of internal motivation.

Even in the darkest hours, you must be able to derive motivation internally; and use that internal motivation to keep moving and keep accomplishing your goals.

Tonight, instead of closing the curtains all the way and jamming a towel under the door to block out any light from creeping in, leave the curtains partly open. Allow the light streaming in through the window to gradually wake you up tomorrow morning before your alarm clock even goes off. Allowing natural light to wake you up gradually each morning can go a long way in terms of synchronizing your internal clock. This could improve your mood significantly, making it easier for you to get and stay motivated. It could also ensure that you stay happy throughout the morning.

Sometimes, when all else fails, caffeine is the answer. Whether you drink coffee, tea, or soda, it may be a good idea to grab one if your energy has flat-lined; and your motivation has disappeared with it. Of course, this strategy will not solve severe motivational problems in the long term, but in the short term, it can go a long way to help you get through the rest of a work day or to help you push through a difficult project.

While many people think to re-organize their offices, less think about reorganizing their computer. In fact, this can go a long way towards ensuring that you stay motivated throughout the day and achieve the goals you have set forth. The reason for this is simple: if you have a disorganized desktop and a disorganized folder structure, you will have a harder time finding things that you need.

The longer it takes you to put together the materials you need for a project, the less you will feel inclined to do so. Restructuring your folders and clearing off your desktop can solve this problem. It will make it easy and convenient for you to find everything, eliminating the incentive to give up and move on.

Life is filled with distractions of many varieties. Having a disorganized workspace can be a distraction. Responding to an email later, rather than sooner, can be a distraction. Leaving a personal issue unresolved can be a distraction. Every loose-end left untied and every issue delayed indefinitely can leave you distracted. And these distractions can kill your motivation, leaving you uninterested and unable to achieve your goals.

For this reason, you should spend some time each day eliminating distractions. Do you have meetings coming up, but you are not sure when they are going to be? Figure it out and put them on your calendar. Do you have emails to send and calls to make? Send the emails and make the calls now. By the end of the day, you will feel less distracted, more motivated, and more able to achieve your goals.

Re-evaluating your life and your goals is not an easy thing to do. It requires a great deal of reflection, planning, and careful thought and who you truly are and what it is that you want to accomplish with the one life that you have.

These are not trivial questions by any means; and so you should ask and answer them carefully.

Spend some time to do this on a monthly or bi-monthly basis. Reacquaint yourself with your life and your goals; and use them to draw motivation for the steps you will have to take next. When it comes to getting motivated, there are few better things you can do than meditation.

Meditation will help you to attain a focus that you may have never achieved in your lifetime thus far. Meditation will allow you to focus so clearly and so carefully on one topic that many challenges and problems you would have noticed otherwise will fade into the background. I personally suggest that you try meditating next time you are feeling unmotivated. If it works for you, keep it in your arsenal of tools, so that you can use it whenever you hit a snag.

It is important for you to find commitment devices that work for you; and to employ them to keep you motivated and to ensure that you have the incentives to reach your goal. One highly effective commitment device is to post your goals publicly. You can do this in a forum, on your blog, or you can simply announce them to your family members and friends. Doing this will make it harder for you to give up on your goals, as you will be held accountable by your blog visitors, by the forum visitors, and by people you know.

If you truly want to accomplish your goals, you have to start by getting motivated. Without motivation, you simply will not be able to muster up the drive to follow through with your plans, complete your objectives, and eventually reach your goal.

Fortunately, motivation does not have to be something that is hard to come-by. It is almost entirely driven by internal moods and decisions. This means that you have a great deal of control over it; and can change it whenever you desire to get better results. It is just a matter of you making that decision and following through.

Best Modes of Internal Motivation

If you are following a specific type of diet plan, you know that there are times when you may feel discouraged, disheartened, weak, or even hopeless when it comes to losing weight. Dieters who are slow to lose weight can feel very depressed. They might find it hard to smile, might constantly be wearing an unattractive frown on their faces, or might even suffer from insomnia or sleepless nights because of their present dieter's depression. When this happens to you, try to remind yourself that your best source of dieter's internal motivation is your own self. While you are following your dieter's meal guide and dieter's fitness plans, there are a set of activities which you can engage in so that you won't have to have those troublesome periods of dieter lows, which have been mentioned in the statements above.

Crying Helps

In spite of what we read about the counterproductive nature of shedding tears when we are confronted by personal challenges, as simple as the major heading above states: crying helps. The act of shedding tears when you're experiencing an all-time low point while you're following your diet should be perceived as an activity that is good for you and your morale. Weep your dieter's frustrations away; this will be an act of internal motivation that can make you feel better. When we shed tears, we are able to release large amounts of tension, stress, and negativity which are types of psychological and emotional burdens in humans. When you find yourself in tears, jot down your thoughts on paper. Identify the causes of your frustrations while you're shedding tears. You might be able to arrive at a significant number of relevant conclusions about the sources of your dieter's discouraged state. Keep a copy of these thoughts which you've written down; keep these for future reference.

Exercise and Your Hormones

Exercise and various types of physical activities are ways to invite internal motivation. An individual dieter doesn't just need exercise for the purpose of burning the calories in the diet meals that this individual consumes. Exercise also functions as a channel for tension, stress, and negativity release. After your daily exercise routines, you feel renewed, exhilarated, and even ecstatic. Diet exercise routines are great ways to feel good about your self, all over again. These are manners of daily rejuvenation. Through exercise, a person's body is able to reactivate the levels of dormant serotonin which the body keeps stored in one's stream of hormones. When we exercise, we sweat and our perspiration contains harmful toxins from our bodies. These harmful toxins come from the food and drinks that we consume and from the environment; toxins are often the leading causes of hormonal imbalances. Hormonal imbalances and chemical imbalances are directly related to depression in people. Through exercise, we're able to treat the major causes of our dieter's fatigue and other types of diet symptoms. Here's an added piece of advice: try not to cry too much and don't over exercise. Indeed, crying and exercise are effective forms of internal motivation, but it's good to remember that all things good are best with moderated use.

EMPATHY

Generally, we define empathy as the ability to sense emotions of others coupled with the ability to judge what someone else might be thinking and feeling. In common parlance, empathy is most often defined by the metaphors: 'standing in someone else's shoes' or 'seeing through someone else's eyes'

Psychologically speaking, there are basically four kinds of empathy in humans, which are self-empathy, mirror (emotional) empathy, cognitive empathy and compassionate empathy as described below:

- Self empathy - Self-empathy is the act of giving ourselves empathy, listening to our own feelings and unmet needs with compassion and understanding. This does not make the problems go away, or magically make all our needs met. But it does help us to feel connected and centered within ourselves. It can also be a tool to express ourselves with more honesty. Though it doesn't make problems go away, it makes it easier to endure them.

- Cognitive empathy - It means knowing how the other person feels and what they might be thinking. It is very helpful in negotiations or motivating people. It has been found that people who possess good cognitive empathy (also called perspective taking) make good leaders or managers because they are able to move people to give their best efforts. But there can be a downside to this type of empathy. If people, falling within the "Dark Triad" - narcissists, Machiavellians and psychopaths - possess ample ability of cognitive empathy, they can exploit others to the extent of torturing them. Such people have no sympathy for their victims and expertly use their ability to calibrate their cruelty.

- Emotional empathy - It means feeling physically along with the other person as though their emotions are contagious. It makes one well-attuned to another's emotional world, which is a plus in any of the wide range of callings. There is a downside attached to emotional empathy that occurs, when people lack the ability to manage their own emotions. This can be seen as psychological exhaustion leading to a burnout as commonly seen in professionals. The purposeful detachment cultivated by those in medical profession is a way to void burnout. But when the detachment leads to indifference, it can seriously hamper the professional care.

- Compassionate empathy - Also commonly referred to as empathic concern, this type of empathy not only means understanding a person's predicament and feel with them but spontaneously move to help them, if needed. In fact, empathic concern is the vital ingredient of an empathic response in a given situation. It is the kind most required in people working as social volunteers.

Empathy - a basic trait -

Empathy is inherently present in humans to varying extents and, therefore, we are affected by another's predicament differently. In fact, it is one of the basic traits of humans so much so that any one devoid of it strikes us as dangerous or mentally ill.

Females frequently score higher on standard tests of empathy, social sensitivity, and emotion recognition than do males.

Its inherence in humans can be established by the fact that how young children respond to the emotions of family members. Besides children, some household pets also express their worry, when the family members are in distress. The pets hover nearby and put their heads in their owners' laps showing that even animals have empathy. Besides humans, many other species exhibit presence of empathy to a varying extent.

A compelling evidence for the presence of empathy in animals came from the following research. The researchers reported in 1964 in the American Journal of Psychiatry that rhesus monkeys refused to pull a chain that delivered food to themselves if doing so gave a shock to a companion. One monkey stopped pulling the chain for 12 days after witnessing another monkey receive a shock. Those primates were literally starving themselves in order to avoid causing hurt to other animals.

Role of empathy in life -

- Empathy plays great role in our life in almost every sphere. The skill of empathy, though we inherit it, can be cultivated, which plays a significant role in making us successful in those spheres. Role of empathy in the life of an individual is actually dependent on its conceptualization by the individual, which varies widely. Nevertheless, empathy acts to reflect what has been perceived and creates a supportive or confirming atmosphere.

- Empathy is a powerful communication skill that is actually underused by many. It allows one to understand thoughts and resultant feelings created by them in others. Empathy also makes one to respond to other's feelings sympathetically so that they can win their trust, which promotes communication further. Our fear of failure, anger, and frustration suddenly drop away, allowing for a more meaningful dialogue and a deepening of relationships.

- Empathy is more than simple sympathy, which makes the individual understand others with compassion and sensitivity. That is why it is plays an important role in the workplace, where many people work together to achieve something of significance. It helps create deep respect for the co-workers, thereby fostering a harmonious atmosphere in the workplace.

- Similarly, empathy is helpful in our professional life because, besides facilitating communication, it makes us a sympathetic listener to our clients, whereby we are able to understand them better.

- Because empathy makes us able to communicate effectively and listen empathetically, we stand a better chance of making our personal and social relationships successful. In fact, empathy is capable of nurturing every kind of relationship we enter into or are in.

- As it is clear that empathy affects our life with far reaching ramifications, we should help our children to cultivate this trait so that they can become better human beings. Since empathy promotes pro-social behavior, it will help our children build close relationships, maintain friendships and develop better communities. Emotional intelligence has assumed great importance over the past twenty years as an instrument in developing an ability to work with our own and other's emotions. One of the most important components of emotional intelligence skills is empathy.

Undoubtedly, empathy immensely affects our everyday life. This trait will come in handy in situations, where we find ourselves trapped, because it will make us understand other's perspectives.

Though we are born with this trait, it happens to be underused by many. As empathy is one of the most important skills to be practiced for success in everyday life, we should encourage our children to cultivate it.

Empathy is an inherent trait in humans but it is present in variable extent in us. That is why everyone doesn't empathize to others to the same extent and in the same manner. Nevertheless, it plays a significant role in our day-to-day life, contributing extensively to our personal, professional and social success.

How do you have empathy? In many cases it comes naturally. In others it helps to take some conscious steps to promote your empathy for others. You need to make it your intention in these cases. Be clear as you face a situation that you want to have empathy for the other person, even if you disagree with them.

Empathy does not necessarily mean agreement. You might want to say that up front. For example, you could say, "I don't expect I shall agree with your position. However, I do want to hear you out and understand you fully." This prepares the other person for the likely outcome. If you do not do this, some people may mistake your good listening for agreement with them.

Once you are clear that you intend to have empathy, you consciously try to put yourself in the other person's shoes. What does it look like and feel like from their point of view? Even more importantly, what values do they embrace? What is important to them? That is the bull's eye, the crucial item for you to understand and have empathy for.

Asking yourself these questions will put you on the right track. You are living out your intention to have empathy when you focus your mind on answering these questions. This also helps you be a better listener. Your mind has lots of extra horse power when you are listening because your mind can work much faster than the other person can speak. Your mind can process 1000 words per minute, but people only speak about 180 words per minute. What to do with that extra horse power or brain power? Harness it to reflect on the above questions. This helps your avoid daydreaming that distracts you from listening.

It helps to temporarily suspend your judgment about their thinking, their positions. You do not need to have empathy about their positions as long as you are seeking to have empathy for their feelings and values. Expressing your judgments about their thinking can come later. Postponing this is a radical new skill for most people. Most people jump right in to argue over positions and try to change the other person's views. Hold off on that until you first achieve empathy.

You can ask yourself the above questions before you enter a crucial conversation. This prepares you to have empathy when you are with the person or on the phone. Don't try to have crucial conversations via email. Then during the conversation, ask the person questions to help them express their feelings and values. When they do, express your empathy.

SOCIAL SKILLS

Having great social skills can open up so many opportunities in the game of life. You can use these skills in so many ways in your life for great rewards. Whether it is on a date with that special someone you just met or to improve yourself in the work place. The rewards can be endless when it comes to having great social skills in life. If you are one of those people that do not benefit from having great social skills you are missing out. There are so many ways to benefit from having good skills for social functions and events.

Just think to yourself What if you could go out somewhere anywhere for that matter and start making new friends. You could benefit from that by having new people to hangout with. With out having social skills you might be to shy to start talking to new people or you lack in confidence to strike up a conversation with someone new.

Have you ever went to a party before and kind of hide in the background? Not knowing how to start a conversation with that nice looking person you have been admiring from across the room. By improving your skills you would have the confidence to walk over there and start talking. Then think of the attention you would develop from everyone else there. You will be laughing and talking meeting new people in no time. Don't you think that would be better then hiding out in the background.

We need to be aware of what we are feeling in order to be aware of our behavioural responses to those feelings or emotions. Once that is in place we can then take responsibility for our responses and manage that behaviour in order to reduce the impact it has upon others and ultimately ourselves. (This is the essence of

Cognitive Behavioural Therapy) We need to understand about our own responses to pain, anger, even love and all our other emotions in order to act appropriately towards other people and ourselves.

The truth is that the most successful people in work and in life have the ability to manage themselves and manage their relationships with others.

Social and emotional intelligence encompasses many skill sets, including stress management, resilience, managing conflict productively, powerful influencing skills, catalysing change, teamwork and collaboration, building trust and much more.

Developing good social skills can be scary at first but once you start you will not want to stop. You slowly start building that confidence level of talking more and getting comfortable in those situations you normally would be uncomfortable in. The stress you would normally face starts going away and you feel better about yourself.

Nothing happens over night it does take work to improve on these skills and the benefits are endless. Everyone has there own reasons to improve these skills. A few simple things you can do to improve on your social skills are work on your body language. Try not to look intimidated or scared when you approach people for the first time. Don't forget to smile. Be polite nobody likes rude people. Find out what interests them and build a conversation around it. Look them in the eyes when your talking. These are just a few things you can do to improve yourself.

Having adequate social skills is a necessity to survive the dating scene, a professional environment and even the everyday family life. From as early as the time that you were a kid, do you remember your mother telling you about how you should behave properly in a social scene or in front of strangers or new acquaintances? With these constant reminders, you would already have a clue about how important it is for a person to learn about social skill development.

There are three basic aspects of social skill development that a person can work on. To have a deeper understanding of how important it is to work on your social skill development, here are the three aspects of social skill development and what you can do to improve them:

1. Verbal Communication

Being an effective communicator is an asset that many would like to have but only a few actually achieve. In lieu of the fact that public speaking is the number one fear of a lot of people not just in the States but around the world - how can you not be afraid of speaking out in front of a large crowd - or worse, in front of a stage? Thus, the first thing that you need to work on for your social skill development is your skill in verbal communication.

If you cannot take the leap and immediately try public speaking, you can take it one small step at a time. Try making small talk with your boss or a person who really intimidates you. Have a casual chat with neighbors or people that you often see. Sharing jokes with them or even greeting them a good day will gradually improve your daily interactions with other people and your verbal communication skill will slowly improve.

If you know how to express yourself clearly, without stuttering or making nervous gestures, then people will warmly respond and you will make them feel comfortable when they see that you yourself are comfortable with the social situation that you are in.

2. Non-verbal Communication

Another skill that you need for social skill development is non-verbal communication. Start with your own gestures. When speaking with another person, you need to look relaxed and not too stiff with your posture, lean a little towards the person that you are speaking with to show them that you are listening, and always have a ready and polite smile.

Next, you need to be aware of the body language of the person that you are speaking with. Never attempt physical contact if you feel that your actions may be misinterpreted. Look for gestures or body movements so that you will see if they are feeling comfortable with your presence. Basically, a relaxed stance should be your clue that the other person is willing to talk with you. Finally, your body language should 'agree' with the words coming out of your mouth.

3. Social Interaction Skills

To further enhance your social skill development, you need to be able to identify and diplomatically resolve any conflict that may arise. If you are embroiled in a tense situation, you should use your diplomatic skills to clear the air. Also, you need to be able to recognize the appropriate behavior so that you will be able to adapt to all sorts of personalities that you will encounter in any social setting.

By learning about these three aspects of social skill development, you can gracefully handle yourself in any social setting so that you can broaden your social circle while at the same time enhancing your interpersonal relationships with other people.

Improving social skill can be said to be dependent on your way of interacting with a person. It involves speaking and listening to a certain topic that both parties wish to discuss. Speaking is as important as listening when it comes to improving social skill.

Some people are especially gifted with the right social skills. They are socially inclined to have the right ways of speaking, listening, and receiving messages. These people are very fortunate to have great social skills. People require basic knowledge of social skills because it is the primary way of communicating to others. It is dependent on verbal and nonverbal communication.

Verbal communication is a way of communicating with words, while nonverbal communication involves body language such as nodding, smiling, frowning and even the use of sign language (if you happen to be deaf).

Just as there are people who have good social skills, there are also people who are beset by problems with speaking and even listening. The results of poor social skills may lead one to become a loner with low self-esteem who is always being left out of discussions.

Proven Ways of improving social skill:

1 Try helping yourself first before asking others for their assistance. You can practice your social skill through daily situations such as going to work, shopping, talking with friends, chitchatting with family members and discussing work with colleagues.

2   Using a mirror can make you more self aware (compared to just speaking with a real person where you study the reactions of another person rather than yourself.)

By practicing, you will notice that you will eventually become comfortable with speaking with another person in no time. Even the nonverbal ways of communication (such as nodding, smiling, other facial expressions, and even body language) will then come automatically.

3   However, you should also be aware that nonverbal communication starts with involuntary actions. While talking with someone over a funny topic, you tend to smile unknowingly. For instance, agreeing with a speaker will make you nod. These are nonverbal ways of communicating. It comes naturally from a person without needing to be reminded.

4   Receiving information is also crucial. Getting the right message is proof of how well you can communicate. The fact that you always try to listen but somehow always get the wrong impression is a sign of weak social skills. Try to be a better listener so that receiving information becomes very easy.

5   Some social skill help can be found around you, if you think you need it. A family member can help you out anytime you ask. A good friend may also attempt to provide feedback on your level of social skill in a way that will not leave you embarrassed.

6   If your poor social skills is uite severe, there are social skill classes that may help you, particularly in communication. Classes are offered both for children and for adults. There are social skill deficiencies manifested by common

disorders called ADHD (Attention Deficit Hyperactivity Disorder) and ADD (Attention Deficit Disorder) which manifest as early as in pre-school age children.

Schools for social skill building offer help with communication and relationship skills such as listening, conversing, reading and using proper body language, managing social interaction and peer relationships, developing self-control and self-esteem, getting along with other people and making friends, handling teasing and many more. Choose a program that is designed to fit your needs.

Learning these skills will enhance your chances for more successful social interaction. You will establish social competence, self-esteem and positive communication skills. It is very important to build communication skills as early as possible to create a good foundation for interacting with others.

CHAPTER 3

THE CHECKLIST TO FIND OUT IF YOU'RE EMOTIONALLY INTELLIGENT

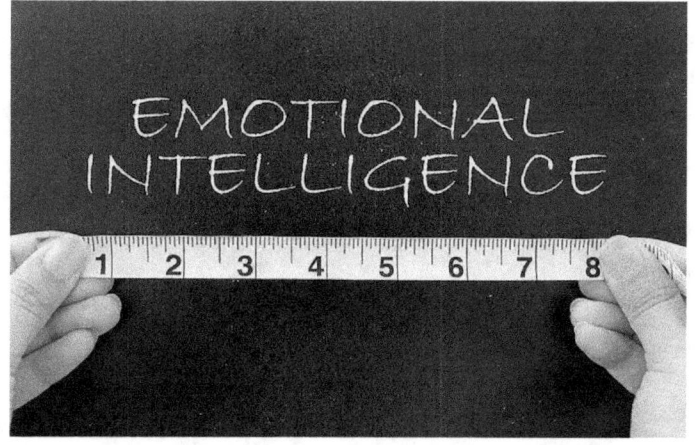

Are you an emotionally intelligent person? Do you know how to control your thoughts and emotions?

Understand your feelings and desires

Most people who are honest with themselves and who know what they want, and know how to express their feelings properly are usually the happiest people and the least vulnerable to become depressed. These are the people who usually succeed in making productive relationships with others because they depend heavily on expressing their feelings in every social relationship they have, hence they are usually the most emotionally intelligent people.

Understand and know yourself more

Now, you know what you want and what your desires are, but let me ask you something. Do you know exactly why you want the goals you have chosen? Do you realize how these emotions will impact your behavior and actions?

Learn to control your emotions

Learning to control your emotions is an important skill that you have to acquire to help you avoid difficult situations that you might experience in life. It will also protect you from listening to destructive emotions that may destroy your life. How to control your emotions?

To be able to control your emotions, you have to learn to control your thoughts first as emotions are the results of your thoughts. No one can have an emotion without having a thought first. Therefore, it is crucial that you learn to control your thoughts, so you can control your emotions.

For every thought that you experience, there is always at least two interpretations, one positive and one negative. If a thought pops up into your mind, it is up to you to decide on which interpretation you choose, why not choose the positive one?

Always remember what Dave Lennick said, "Emotional competence is the single most important personal quality that each of us must develop and access to experience a breakthrough. Only through managing our emotions can we access our intellect and our technical competence. An emotionally competent person performs better under pressure.

How High is Your Team's Emotional Intelligence (EQ)?

Emotional Intelligence (EQ) is usually described in terms that apply to individuals. It describes how well someone is able to recognize, manage, and use their own emotions effectively. High EQ is essential to managing your own behavior effectively and to build and maintain strong interpersonal relationships with others.

EQ not only applies to individuals, but also to teams, groups, and even entire organizations. While most people know what high EQ looks like in a person, there are also clear signs that can help you to recognize the functioning EQ level of your own work group, team, and even your entire organization.

How High EQ in Teams & Groups Yields Increased Performance ?

High EQ teams are easy to spot because they demonstrate high levels of interpersonal competency across a wide range of day-to-day interactions. These are groups that work together to create high levels of trust, leverage conflict to produce good decisions, and hold each other accountable to produce and deliver outstanding results.

High EQ team members are not "divas" or "lone wolves." They are equally committed to each team member's success as much as they are to their own. They recognize that team members are interdependent upon each other for success. One of the clearest signs of a high EQ group is that tough issues get surfaced and resolved.

Conflict is seen as an ordinary and necessary part of problem solving. Important issues are passionately debated and discussed, but there are clear ground rules in place to contain any untoward emotional outbursts or personal attacks. Instead, honest dialogue and debate is used to address important issues.

High EQ teams also display a clear sense of commitment that leads to an alignment that focuses on achieving goals and outcomes. If team members do get sidetracked or derailed then other team members use accountability to get the stray member back on track or they surface the issue to the rest of the team or to leadership for an intervention. But, they do not let status and ego get in the way of teams delivering results.

High EQ Signs in Groups, Teams, and Organizations

- ❖ Team members trust each other enough to openly talk about their own strengths and weaknesses.
- ❖ Honest conflict is viewed as necessary and even desirable for effective decision-making.
- ❖ Passionate debate and discussion is used to generate alternative ideas and approaches so that the best course of action can be chosen from those created during open debate and dialogue.
- ❖ Senior organizational leaders are self-aware of their own power and influence

and use appropriate self-control to regulate their own emotions as to have optimal communication with others. For example, they may wait to speak last at a meeting so that their comments do not stifle a more thorough and open discussion.

❖ Supervisors and managers demonstrate high levels of integrity and are trusted even though others may sometimes disagree with them about specific actions or decisions.

❖ Negative feedback is not avoided, but it is delivered to members in a way that preserves their professional pride and self-esteem as to assure continued employee engagement and positive motivation.

❖ The process used to achieve the outcome is as equally important as the outcome itself. Producing high results through unacceptable behavior does not meet the expected standard. The ends do not justify the means.

❖ Members can readily accept responsibility for their actions and they understand how their behavior, decisions, and reactions will resonate across other team members.

❖ Team members establish clear down ground rules for unacceptable behavior and the standards are well known to all. For example, problem solving is focused on learning from mistakes and not just assigning blame.

❖ Team members hold each other accountable, confront unacceptable behavior, and share credit for team success and achievements.

Why Low EQ in Teams and Groups Often Sabotages Success

Low EQ teams also show their own unique signs and styles. However, these behaviors tend to interfere with teams and organizations from being able to effectively deal with tough issues.

Low EQ teams often have fits and starts of success and emotional outbursts, especially when a crisis occurs. This affective instability often results in teams that produce inconsistent results.

Low EQ teams have members that often feel insecure, lack management competency, and tend to see conflict as a sign of dysfunction. Team members often dread meetings and their group interactions are characterized by an active avoidance of conflict and leave members with high levels of stress from leaving important issues unresolved.

Team members are unlikely to take bold risks or encourage other members to do so. Low EQ team members become experts at creating "pre-emptive" excuses so they can readily shift blame away from themselves when the team consistently fails to deliver results.

There is often a tacit agreement between members not to hold each other accountable so that team problems can be externalized to outside forces or unforeseen circumstances. This protects everyone's ego and status and does not force team members to examine how their own interactions propagate low performance and failing to deliver the results and goals expected.

Signs of Low EQ in Groups, Teams, & Organizations

- ❖ Team members are reluctant to openly admit their own weaknesses or mistakes and will rarely ask for help, even if it is clearly needed.

- ❖ Team members are reluctant to hold each other accountable to their commitments and responsibilities for fear that it may damage interpersonal relationships and others may then also hold them accountable.

- ❖ Fragile egos of senior leaders lead to "out of bounds" or "forbidden" topics that need to be addressed, but cannot because team members feel unsupported challenging the ineffective pet policies of key players.

- ❖ Individual competition and the need for high individual achievement often interfere with necessary cooperation and teamwork necessary to create the collaboration needed to create win-win solutions.

- ❖ Members are unwilling or incapable of passionate debate about critical issues, unless a crisis is looming, and then the conflict becomes personal and ineffective.

❖ Artificial Harmony exists among team members whenever powerful outside players are present. Everyone seems to get along swell when the regional vice-president is visiting.

❖ Time and energy are actively invested in avoiding conflict and directed toward shifting blame and responsibility onto others. "Pre-emptive" excuses and other ways to avoid accountability are freꞯuently used to protect status and egos.

❖ Fear of making a "bad" decision often results in "analysis paralysis" and constant delays which prevent team members from taking decisive action. The need for a "perfect" solution gets in the way of an "effective" solution.

❖ Negative feedback is delivered inconsistently and often in a way that is not constructive. There are emotional outbursts and team members are made scapegoats for poor leadership.

❖ Team members often feel that they are being humiliated or embarrassed, while more senior managers see them as being too sensitive and needing a thicker skin.

❖ Organizational leaders do not accept responsibility for any issues relating to culture or morale. The problem is always with the person or the team and never with the organization or the culture.

What to Do If You Need to Raise Your Group's EQ?

If you are fortunate enough to belong to a high EQ team, then you already know what it feels like to be part of a successful group, team, or organization. If, however, you see your team acting in Low EQ ways, then you need to decide what you can do to make things better.

It's very important to realize that improving the EQ level of a group or team is a much tougher task than working with a single low performing team member. This is because you are dealing with group dynamics, different levels of interpersonal functioning, and a collection of egos and people who are likely to be fearful of change and doubt their own ability to improve. After all, they have developed a number of ineffective ways at deflecting responsibility and accountability, so don't expect them to welcome and opportunity to resolve the conflicts they have been actively avoiding.

The first place to start in developing higher group EQ is to assess where your team is functioning well now and where there is a clear need for professional development. Do not attempt do this job alone - get help. Locate either an internal or external expert who has experience in working with EQ and groups.

Work with your expert to establish exactly what behaviors are contributing to success and what behaviors are interfering with reaching team goals. Then figure out a set of strategies to advance team development around the core issues of trust, conflict management, commitment, and accountability. Remember, change is a process and not an event. Even with expert help, it may take 6-12 months of active focus before you see significant improvement

I can tell you, from personal experience, that it is possible to increase a team's EQ. But, it absolutely requires a strong and secure team leader who is able to recognize the signs of low EQ and how it is negatively affecting performance. The team leader must also be willing to ask for help, accept outside advice and counsel, and be willing to support ongoing change.

The expert and the team leader, working together, must develop ways for team members to hold each other accountable and for letting go of the old ways of interacting. Conflict avoidance must be abandoned and teams must be shown how to effectively integrate conflict into normal problem solving to achieve better results. Team members must be taught how to give and receive honest feedback in ways that address real issues. Finally, all team members must feel empowered enough to challenge members who lose focus or do not deliver on their commitments.

Not all teams can make the change from low EQ to high EQ. It's tough, takes hard work, and challenges the usual way of interacting. But, for those teams that are able to raise their EQ, they often find that they are capable of far more effective problem solving than they ever believed possible. High EQ team members have high levels of engagement, produce more high quality results, and are committed to their team and organization. Finally, high EQ teams often become talent magnets and attract top level talent across all levels of the organization.

CHAPTER 4

FAILSAFE STEPS TO DEVELOP
SOLID SELF-AWARENESS

Why is it easier to grasp the essence of the problem when it is not you causing the dispute between two people? It becomes almost a second nature to see the simplicity of the cause; however, once you find yourself involved, you struggle to resolve the issues. Your self-awareness gets blurry by the circumstances you are facing in the heat of the moment.

At that moment, you will struggle to see how your behaviour and irrational thinking manipulate your ability to have clarity. Self-awareness is a powerful way to distinguish yourself as who you are and what you want to become. In many ways, that can be blinded if you accept life's problems to control the outcome of your life.

Everyone has this terrific capability to evaluate their success and achieve a greater life; however, not everyone chooses to use it! There is a secret to increase your ability to be more aware of what you want in life, and how to get it.

That secret can enhance specific areas in your life remarkably quickly, and it all boils down to the power of asking the right questions. These

Questions will give you the right answers to overcome the barriers you struggle with in life. It is only when you start becoming the "outsider" of your own existence and looking in, that you will be able to regulate where necessary.

Self-Awareness is a way of looking into our own consciousness and seeing how we are responding to the world around us. Its a personal progress report that can tell us how we are functioning mentally, physically, and emotionally. Being aware of oneself is the ultimate freedom, giving us control over our values, beliefs, and destinations. Being self-aware is the key to unlocking a better you, and the discovery of a life fully lived. Finally making peace with who you are, where you are, and where your going will set you up to be truly happy and give you the boldness you need to conquer many of life's obstacles.

The benefits of being self-aware are numerous, in which the most important are: acting on facts and not feelings, the capability to love yourself, developing real and better relationships, accomplishing goals, avoid repeat mistakes, and obtaining the proper knowledge to change your bad habits and behaviors.

When you really think about it, self-awareness is a necessity for creating any positive change in your life, and developing good habits that will last. How can we change a behavior or fix a problem if we don't know what is wrong? The journey to being in tune with you is not easy, but will be very rewarding, and the hard work you put in will reap many benefits. Let's take a look at the 5 steps to discovering the real you.

<u>REMOVE</u>

The first stop on the journey to self-reflection and awareness is removing obstacles, distractions, and temptations that cloud our minds on a daily basis. We find many excuses to not confront ourselves, and reasons not take a closer look at how the events of our world and actions of people make us feel. Taking a deep look into the mirror is hard, and the number one reason is fear. We are afraid that what we see will not be something we like, or that it will be disappointing, ugly, etc. Because this is so hard, we need to take the proper steps in making reflection as easy as possible, and this means removing anything in the way.

Why must we keep busy 24/7, especially in this paced-paced we are living in today? Its almost as if we view slowing down as a negative thing that is a sign of laziness, but I would say being to busy to check in with one's self is very damaging and can lead to discontentment. If you are like me, you are over-committing yourself, and need tools to help remove things to give you time to reflect. Here are ways to help you remove the clutter of the mind body, and soul.

1 Unplug: Technology has taken control of our lives, and unless you take very focused action, you will be distracted by calls, texts, emails, tweets, pins, etc. Set yourself limits on how long you will be on the computer, how many times you will check your email on your phone, and make strict TV rules. Set a designated time each night to turn off your phone and not take calls or check email.

2 Just Say No: Saying yes has become a disease most of us are infected with. We want to please our friends, family, co-workers, and show everyone how

awesome we are. Over committing is a sure fire way to burn out, and will leave you with hardly anytime to work on yourself. Saying no feels bad in the moment, but will lead to a better healthier you who is able to accomplish the things you do with quality.

3   Meditate: Meditation is a concentrated effort that focuses on clearing your mind completely; it's like pushing the reset button for your thoughts. Meditation focuses on breathe and the complete removal of all mind matters, the goal being able to obtain inner peace and allow to start with a clean slate. Think of it as wiping the mind's canvass so you can start with a fresh and clean one to paint with. When we remove negative thoughts, thoughts of fear and doubt, we can begin to shift our thinking into something more positive and productive.

REFLECT

After we have cleaned the "room" of our mind, and eliminated distractions and unhealthy emotions, it's time to actually take a look inside to see what is really there; its time to reflect. Reflection is the dirty business; it exposes the dirty laundry and areas we would like to improve in. Reflection can also surprise us, there are things we may be proud of or areas we have made tremendous progress and personal growth. Self-reflection is taking the time to just think about your life and the journey you are on, and how you feel about the current state. Are you happy, are you engaged in activities that reflect your values, and are you living a life that you are proud of? These are just a few of the questions we should ask ourselves along the reflective process.

The 8 Questions To Ask While Engaging in Self-Reflection

1. Am I Staying True To My Core Values?

2. Am I Someone Others Respect?

3. Do I respect myself?

4. Am I Living Up To My Potential?

5. Am I Engaging In The Activates and Hobbies I Like?

6. Am I Giving My Best To Those That Matter?

7. What Is My Impact In The World?

8. Where Does My Current Path Lead?

<u>REACT</u>

After we have cleared the mind of distractions, and reflected on what is happening inside the heart and soul, the next step is to react. What I mean by reaction is sitting with the way your mind Processes the questions you have just asked yourself. In essence, the classic therapist line, "how does that make you feel". This brings us to something called the "Emotional Response", and is crucial, but only part of the reactive response of self-reflection. Reactions are your indicators that some changes may need to take place down the road, or perhaps that you are on the right track, and it merely re-centered your efforts. It would be a good idea to write down the answers to the questions you just went through so that you remember the way you felt, and can remember for the next time you sit down to reflect.

The mental reaction to reflecting can be very emotional, and prepare yourself to feel things you haven't felt in a while, maybe anger towards an ex-boss or spouse, or sadness over a tragedy you never quite healed from. These are things of the past that need healing, and confronting them is the first step. You may also feel you need to change things that you can control in the present, and this will lead us to the next step in the self-awareness journey.

__RESPOND__

After you sit with the mental reaction to the discovery of well. Yourself, the next step is responding with action, implementing steps for healing, change, or closing unfinished business. Responding to things is another way of saying dealing with them. Dealing with issues that come up during self-reflection is a step towards inner peace and moving on, and becoming the person you desire to be. There are several core responses that will bring healing and positive change, lets discuss the 3 things you will need to start the change process.

1 Forgive Others: Odds are you have realized you hold bitterness, sadness, or aggression against something or someone that came up during your self-aware process. Humans hurt people, and everyone gets let down, and sometimes

we are hurt very badly. Pain and bitterness shape the way we respond to daily activities and can even shape the way we view life. Because of this it is important to let things go, and let the past be the past. Don't let others control you, choose to free yourself and move on.

2 Forgive Yourself: One of the hardest parts of being us, is the fact that we let ourselves down, and make mistakes. Welcome to humanity, you are not alone. Mistakes are important teachers, they are guides of sorts, to steer us closer to the direction we want to go. Learn your lessons and move on, give up the act of trying to be perfect, instead work on becoming the best you. The best you isn't having a standard of perfection, this only leads to disappointment.

3 List Changes: Make a list of the changes you want to make after the self-evaluation

you have just completed. These changes become goals to keep track of. Make benchmarks for your goals, and keep yourself accountable so you can re-adjust every time you start falling into old patterns.

<u>REPEAT</u>

Practice makes perfect, and becoming self-aware takes many hours of concentrated effort. Write down the steps, questions, and techniques that have worked for you, and form a system of going through the reflection process. Repeating the process means adjusting to goals you have met, or new goals you discover to work on. After a while you will want to evaluate the list you wrote down, and see how you feel about each item. As you grow, feelings can change so don't forget to reflect on the same items regularly. If you have completely conquered the item at hand, happily cross it off and move to other items down the list. Also evaluate if the issue is still relevant to your overall goals, or if you have made some self-discoveries that don't make it necessary to work on. As we experience healing our perspectives change and we may find we feel completely different about something, causing an entirely different emotional reaction. For example, that college girl friend that broke your heart might become a point of happy nostalgia, representing the simpler days of love and not the bitter memory it once was. This will give you a point blank shot of the power changing our own perspective through self-reflection holds.

That was easy right, just remember becoming self-aware takes time and a lot of hard work, and will eventually pay off in a rewarding way. The end goal is becoming the person you want and were meant to be, achieving happiness and peace of mind. There is an enormous joy and freedom that comes with knowing whom you really are, and letting others see the truth will bring relief and comfort. So get to work, master self-awareness, and discover the better you!

CHAPTER 5

EFFECTIVE TIPS TO HELP YOU
UNDERSTAND OTHERS

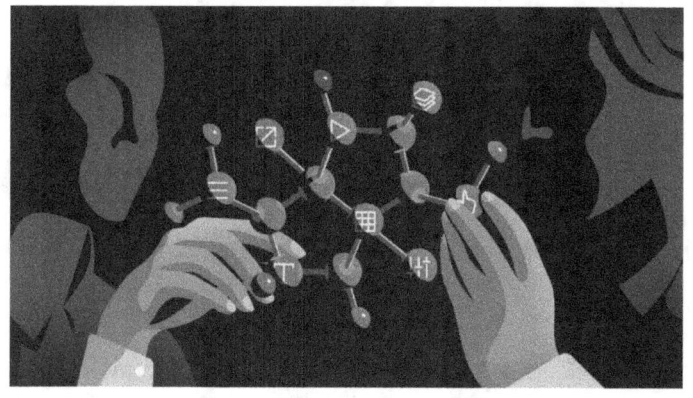

In the highly competitive world of sales it's often all too easy to ignore some of the more subtle skills of salesmanship as the pressure to identify leads, set up meetings and close deals becomes all encompassing. However, it is the finer points of being a salesman, and more importantly in engaging with people, that can lead to more success.

The main core of salesmanship is the ability to engage with and persuade people. Although elements such as age, cultural background, language and individual personality can have a large impact on human interaction, there are some central rules that govern our behaviour and which have a profound effect on whether we immediately feel comfortable engaging with each other. By understanding people, you're in a much better position to push the right buttons to make a deal more likely. The following set of tips will help you to develop a killer toolkit to compliment your sales arsenal and boost your sales career.

KNOW THE PRODUCT

Know your products inside out. Being able to answer any questions on your product will enable you to deal with any negativity or issues head on, and sets a far more professional air. You customers need to buy into you before they can buy into your product. If you don't know what you're talking about you cannot build the trust that you need to persuade that customer further along the sales process.

KNOW THE INDUSTRY

Keep abreast of industry news, spending 20 minutes or so each morning to pick up on the recent headlines, and read a few news articles. All of this can be done online, and just a few minutes worth of research every day will give you an enviable battery of small talk topics for your particular market. For customers, speaking to someone who has a firm grasp on the current events in the industry is another demonstration of their commitment and enthusiasm to the industry, reinforcing your position as a member of your customer's particular group and not as an outsider.

BE PERSONABLE

Humans are highly visual, and a well presented person is instinctively trusted more than they more dishevelled competitor. When meeting clients dress for the occasion, be presentable, smart and ensure that you pay attention to the small details, all of which can help set you aside from the competition and make a more powerful first impression.

It's very easy to try to adopt a persona that you think a client will like, but be aware that false personas are very easy to spot since they are so very unnatural. There are natural body language pointers that identify if you are lying or being deceptive, and adopting a false persona will start setting off these signals. Be approachable, open, and amenable. Listen to what your customer is telling you, and use that information later on to help communication further. Don't try to be someone that you're not, but instead focus on being someone that the customer feels they can talk to.

GIVE THINGS AWAY

At the start of any sales process customers will naturally be guarded and distrusting, it's natural human behaviour. Having some news articles, web links to useful information or other such resources can really help to demonstrate your willingness to help your customer as a whole, not just in making a sale. The resources should be related to the industry that your customer operates in, but perhaps not relevant to the sale you're trying to make. Being helpful outside of the sales process demonstrates that you're not just after the customer's money, but in developing a good professional relationship.

GO THAT EXTRA MILE

When attending a meeting do some extra research to find out a little more about your customer or their company. This will help you stand out amongst the competition and can help a customer feel more valued.

Answer all calls in the timeliest fashion possible and deliver on any and all promises that you make to a customer. This is the best trust building tool that you have. A customer cannot buy from someone they do not trust. Building trust is the foundation to any ongoing relationship, and starting a commercial relationship off with a high degree of trust will maximise ongoing sales later, so going the extra mile will pay off.

USE THE RIGHT LANGUAGE

All sales people are taught to use open-ended questions to keep a conversation going, one of the most basic communication principles. In addition, using the right words and being mindful of your body language will be crucial in developing a rapport with a potential customer. Often more than 55% of your communication is non-verbal, communicated through your body posture. Adopting a non-threatening, open body language is key to making your customer feel comfortable in your presence. If the customer doesn't feel comfortable then they won't trust you. If they don't trust you, they won't buy from you.

Using the right words will also help you to take shortcuts into a customer's psyche. Using the same terminology as your customer is using can help to position you as part of a group, one of the pack. Using the right terminology indicates that you understand your customer and are not an outsider.

OLD SCHOOL IS BEST SCHOOL

When it comes to human interaction face to face or vocal communication is still the absolute best form. This doesn't mean that there's no place for email or even social media in the world of sales, but technology should be a method for you to manage and source your customers. When it comes to the final stages use the phone and arrange face to face meetings.

HUMAN SCHEDULES

Spend time to understand how your customers structure their day. Are there obvious points during which a phone call from you would be more welcome? Is sending an email at a certain time likely to end in it being deleted or even plain ignored because you've sent it at the peak activity time of the day?

Understand how your customers schedule their daily activities and plan your day around this. Don't call customers when they're likely to be at their busiest, and don't be prospecting for new leads when your current leads are more willing and able to take a call from you!

NLP

Studying the basics of NLP, or Neuro Linguistic Programming, can help you to make your own communication with customers far more effective by giving you an insight into the type of person your customer is and how to best structure your words and sentences to make your messages more acceptable to that customer. Study NLP and fully embrace what it offers.

TIPS FOR READING PEOPLE'S THOUGHTS

The idea of reading the thoughts of other people, has been one of those things that has been a topic of discussion for many years. Indeed reading other people's thoughts is one of those things that everyone has encountered many times during life. Many times you may have been thinking about a close friend or a loved one, and the next thing is that they call you on the phone or visit you. It could be easy to call things like this coincidence but if we consider that there may be more to this universe than meets the eye. So what is the truth about reading other people's thoughts? And is it possible to read the thoughts of another person?

THE POWER OF COMMUNICATION

It has been said that when you speak, the words only communicate a small percentage of the information. Some of the more important aspects are tone of the voice and body language. Indeed the tone of a persons voice and body language can show when someone is lying. Have you noticed when a person is lying they find it hard to make eye contact, so this points to the fact that spoken communication is not the only way that we communicate. Have you looked at the way that birds fly in perfect formation even though we do not perceive them communicating. So do we have the ability to communicate on a psychic level? And could it be the case that we all have the capacity to communicate on a psychic level?

WHAT CAN WE LEARN FROM THE NEAR DEATH EXPERIENCE?

There was a story of a man who had a near death experience when he was 16 years of age, but had an interesting story about his experience. Following the event he appeared to become more psychic, so when people asked him how did he become psychic he gave this answer. He said that you do not become psychic, you are psychic and you choose to forget you are psychic to make this earth experience more realistic. So could this suggest that we may have the ability to communicate using thought communication, and is this a skill that we can develop? And perhaps we may even be able to develop this by using methods like meditation. I have personally found that I have been able to pick up vague thoughts from my children following meditation. So does psychic abilities have links to the ability to read the thoughts of other people.

GOOD RELATIONSHIPS

It has been found that when people are in close harmony they tend to pick up the thoughts that each other is thinking, this tends to suggest the importance of having a good and close positive relationship. In N L P the suggestion is that by exercises such as matching breathing two people are able to build rapport. So the idea of reading the mind of another person could possibly be initiated by some form of mental permission giving. If this is the case then the idea of reading the thoughts of another person may be associated with the building of trusted relationships. So have you experienced thinking about a close friend and then being contacted by them, and have you found that a close friend has been thinking the same thought that you have been thinking. - Thoughts To Make You Think.

CHAPTER 6

LEADERSHIP AND THE
SECRETS OF MOTIVATION

It is often asked how leaders can better motivate
their employees. This simple question covers lots
of situations and is often a request for strategies
to change another adult's workplace behavior

while assuming he/she is resistant or indifferent to making the change.

There can be a lot going on behind employee under performance or disinterest that a manger may interpret as unmotivated performance. Let's go past tips and tricks for motivating employees and look at the role of conflict, standards and accountability, and goals and talent all play a role in enhancing or inhibiting employee motivation.

Control and Conflict: Imagine a group of professionals who regularly put out sloppy, incorrect, misspelled and poorly punctuated documents. A snap judgment could easily conclude that they are unmotivated. Let's take a closer look into this case study and uncover the dynamics behind this symptom of unmotivated performance.

In a CPA firm I worked with, the owner was very meticulous - good for accounting accuracy - bad for motivated, self-directed employees. For example, each month his firm would send out payroll tax letters to client companies that his employees would draft. He insisted on reviewing these for accuracy. Once he was happy with accounting accuracy, he would then review each letter for grammatical and stylistic elements. He'd correct/modify these in red and send them back for revisions. When corrected by his accountants, he'd review them again, make modifications and send them back again, etc. Ironically, the more he sent back letters for improvement the worse the quality got. They regularly sent him incomplete letters with glaring errors causing him to bring out bigger and bigger red pens. This dumbfounded and aggravated him tremendously.

We had to address the conflict between his need for preferential perfection and his employees' need for feelings of autonomy and ownership in their work. We designed a company meeting to bring out both sides of this conflict on the table. We identified the benefit both employees and management got from keeping the conflict going: the employees could absolve themselves of responsibility and enjoy the game of complaining about the boss as the bad guy, while the owner got to feel that he knew more than his employees did justifying his position and authority. Once acknowledged, neither side wanted to keep this game going. We built a new procedure for handling these letters and all written correspondence in the future.

Control was an issue we continued to work on with the owner through coaching sessions in order to expand and sustain this change toward more employee autonomy and internal motivation. Issues quickly faded because the root cause was not one where motivation was lacking - management control resulting in conflict and employee passive aggressive behavior was.

Standards and Accountability: Often when leaders ask about motivation, what they are really saying is, "How do I get someone who doesn't want to do something to do it?" So, let's take a look at the bottom line of accountability. Motivation or not, there are job elements that are not optional. Routine nonperformance deserves exploration before declaration - the conclusion that the employee is unmotivated. This behavior should actually be described as underperformance, which is measurable, rather than as unmotivated, which is an opinion describing the personal dynamic behind the under-performance.

The employee must be alerted to his inadequate performance and be given a chance to correct it with the support of agreed upon action plans built with his manager. Follow up meetings will support either positive recognition if employee changes are being made according to the action plan or progressive consequences if they are not. Consequences will motivate behavior change where disapproving, blaming or generally hostile lectures will not. Use minor consequences early and consistently so both of you can avoid the more severe ones. If despite this, the employee continues to under-perform, he will behave his way out of his job. And while it is never easy to terminate, with the evidence of his broken commitments to manager supported change, a leader will not lose sleep wondering if it's the right decision.

If you've raised teenagers this progression will sound familiar. Indifference on the part of the offending party escalates the emotional reactivity and loss of control in the authority figure undermining their credibility. Because no effective change occurs and no real consequences are implemented, the guilty party learns their leader is ineffective and all they need do is endure the lecture and nothing much will happen after that. No need to change.

The solution? Apply the 80/20 rule with a calm demeanor and align consequences. Instead of lecturing (her 80), we worked with Marilyn to get the supervisors to describe the problem that gets in the way of their timeliness (their 80). Once identified, she led them to design a solution and then followed up on their implementation of it. Additionally, she let them know that the success of their plan was important because the first step of their progressive discipline system would be implemented if they failed to use it successfully. This increased Frankie and Johnny's ownership of the problem and its solution.

Regular follow-up sessions to positively reinforce Frankie and John's typical early success were used with the dates for subsequent follow-up meetings established at each one. This reinforced that this time the change wasn't optional or would fall off Marilyn's radar screen. Add the follow-up meetings and the minor but real consequences that would be applied if they came in late again and a successful performance change occurred immediately.

Aligning Talent and Goals: Now let's look at motivation from another perspective. Consider that you don't have to motivate a child to eat ice cream. In other words, if the activity is enjoyable, beneficial, or meaningful, there is internal motivation to act. And this internal motivation, once activated, generally becomes self-sustaining. So let's look more carefully at the circumstances on the employees' side that might look like a lack of motivation to the manager. Do we know what the employee enjoys doing (a good indication of talent and therefore, internal motivation and employee success)? Talents are by definition the source of intrinsic motivation. We enjoy working in our talent areas because in them we are naturally good at what we do, find the work to be easy and regularly successful. Is the employee in the right position for his talents to be used and create internal motivation? Does the employee know how his work benefits others in the company, customers, and how it helps the company accomplish its mission and goals?

Gallup research tells us that the ability to link one's individual work to a greater purpose/benefit of the organization produces a happier and smarter employee who will make a better contribution to his organization. Do we know what is meaningful to the employee? In other words do we know why he works beyond putting food on the table? If we can link his/her work to the fulfillment of his dreams, we motivate. Stimulus-Response psychology implies that this is not necessary: all we need do is provide the effective positive and negative reinforcers and we can get anyone to behave as we wish. The difference here is between manipulation/coercion and true motivation, which creates self-sustaining behavior with minimal supervision.

Bill worked in a printing shop of about 100 employees. He was a very successful stripper, no, not that kind. His job in the old days was to physically cut and paste the copy to be printed onto plates that would then be burned and used in the printing process. As technology progressed the company went "computer to plate" eliminating the job of the stripper. Bill's boss Peter was loyal to his employees and so refused to let him go. Bill was given a job at the same pay for sweeping up the shop. Neither was very happy. Peter began to experiment with other positions for Bill and when he said he liked computers, Peter moved him into the graphic design area where he was trained to create the artwork customers needed. Another bomb. Peter asked us to assess Bill's talents and we discovered his like for computers had to do with building them, not using them. So we challenged Peter's loyalty as to its boundaries. Would he be willing to help Bill get his next job outside of the company? Peter was immediately intrigued. He paid for some training for Bill in building computers and then used his contacts to help him get his first job. Bill came back two months later just to thank Peter for helping him find a job he loved. The other employees were of course impressed with the company's commitment to its workers and the work culture of the organization was hugely strengthened.

A good manager builds relationships that are positive and trustworthy. With these in place, employees are free to give direct feedback if the manager is creating conflicts. Managers are free to clearly state expectations while ensuring employees have a set up for success. Supporting employee success also supports managers holding them accountable to their goals. Finally, positive relationships allow managers to discover their employees' talents and dreams and do what they can to align their work with them. Motivation then, is not a technique that special leaders use to magically transform employee performance. It is the natural result of thoughtful, caring, and committed leadership, which strives to create a win for both the organization and the employee.

CHAPTER 7

CRUCIAL IDEAS WHICH HELPS TO AVOID SOCIALLY AWKWARD SITUATIONS

Interacting with others can lead to awkward situations. Misreading things like the other person's body language and making jokes the other party members don't find humorous can make a person want to shy away from socializing with people altogether. Luckily, listed below are five helpful tips to surviving any social encounter.

BODY LANGUAGE

People often times don't convey how they really feel but their actions do whether they are aware of them or not. As a general rule of thumb the things to watch for are: crossing arms over the chest (means that person is feeling guarded and doesn't want any physical contact), tilting of the head to the side (to show interest and active listening, commonly seen more in males than females), shifting weight from side to side (reveals nervousness), avoiding eye contact (shows shyness or lack of self-confidence in oneself), and paying attention to which way a person's eyes are drifting in speech. If the person's eyes move up to the left they are accessing memory and if they drift to the right they are accessing creative thoughts and may not be telling you the truth because they aren't accessing memory at all.

HUMOR

Having a sense of humor is something that not everyone possesses but is certainly appreciated if one does have it. Generally humor can turn any awkward experience into a positive one but even if a person has a serious nature doesn't mean they're not worth knowing. More often than not serious individuals are the most intelligent.

TALKING TOO MUCH OR TOO LITTLE

While it's easy to babble when nervous generally the rule of thumb is that when someone speaks too much it's usually a sign of loneliness or unintelligence (or both) and one who speaks less is usually of higher intelligence and pays more attention to detail. In most social situations it's better to remain thoughtful until knowing the other party better.

<u>LYING</u>

Wouldn't it be nice to know if the person being addressed were speaking honestly? Sometimes being truthful is difficult if it might hurt the other person's feelings. Reading body language is an essential part of being able to tell if a person is being truthful. Be forewarned though that often times people with anxiety issues sometimes display some of these traits while giving honest answers. Observe carefully to piece together the clues. These include but are not limited to: eyes that maintain little to no eye contact, rapid eye movement, hand in front of mouth when speaking, body turned away from person addressing, color-changing complexion (like red in the face and neck).

<u>DEFENSIVENESS</u>

Defensiveness is really something a lot of people witness more in business settings during employee reviews and such. The things to look out for when someone is not listening and isn't open to hearing anything beyond their own opinions are: minimal facial expressions, keeping hand or arm gestures close to the body, eyes maintain little eye contact or look downward, and keeping arms crossed in front of the body.

WAYS TO AVOID AWKWARD MOMENTS WHEN MEETING SOMEONE NEW

Meeting someone for the first time can be very unnerving, whether it is a business client, a date, or someone who approaches you in at a social function. Trying to maintain an interesting conversation, remaining composed, and finding common interests can be extremely difficult, and even those highly skilled in social interaction may step into trouble. Here are a few tips that can help you avoid any uneasiness, or at least keep the awkward moments to a minimum.

<u>KEEP IT LIGHT</u>

When meeting for the first time, you do not know their background, temperament, or personality. Until you have a better idea of who they are, keep the conversation light and simple. You never know what will offend or what subjects are off limits to another individual. A harmless sarcastic joke to you may be interpreted as an insult by someone else. This also applies to physical interaction. Many people are comfortable and open with touching and distance with people in general, however, there are many who are not. Be respectful of the levels of comfort in others, and be careful how you interact. If you want to take the conversation to a deeper level, take notice in the way they talk and move. If their body visibly relaxes, they lean in, or their speaking style seems less restricted, test the waters. Suggest a deeper, possibly more controversial subject, let them know something personal about you, or give them a friendly pat on the back. If you see a positive response, continue on. If you observe unease, take a step back to a lighter subject.

SHARING TOO MUCH
INFORMATION

If the conversation shifts to a deeper topic, be careful about what information you share. Although you may be engaged in a discussion of fine wines with a date, they do not necessarily need to know the details of what you did the last time you drank too much. You may know it was an isolated incident, but your date may see an alcoholic sitting in front of them. In a business setting, you may want to build a rapport by sharing something personal with others, but be careful with what you share. An embarrassing story about yourself can be seen as a story about your reckless behavior to someone else. This tip is not applicable in every situation, sometimes conversations can get very personal without problems. However, when making a first impression, you need to think about what you are saying, and how well the person knows you.

Giving too much in the beginning can not only give the wrong impression, but can also make the person you are talking with uncomfortable.

DO NOT COME ON TOO STRONG

A common mistake in new situations is trying too hard to impress, or moving too fast to create a bond with someone. It is important to be confident, but not boastful. We want other people to know how smart, successful, and funny we are, but by talking at length about these traits or accomplishments that demonstrate these qualities, we are only demonstrating our arrogance. If you are truly confident in these areas, they will show in the conversation.

If you feel a connection with someone, do not assume that it means friendship. You may feel secure enough to get closer to your new acquaintance, however your acquaintance may think otherwise. Do not force a connection. Like tip #1, observe the other person's behavior and speech and determine whether they feel that same connection. Test the waters before jumping in.

USE YOUR SOCIAL GRACES

Occasionally the most competent communicators find themselves in awkward situations. A line is crossed, or a comment is interpreted incorrectly. When you find yourself in this position, the proper response can save you. It is easier than it seems when you know how to react. If you have offended someone, simply apologize, explain you meant no offense, clarify what you meant, and move on. If the other person can tell your apology is sincere, they should be able to move on too. If you have suggested a subject they deem inappropriate, apologize if necessary, change the subject, and let it go. Do not dwell on it. If the person does not want to discuss something, most likely they do not want to hear an endless apology on it either.

HAVE AN EXIT STRATEGY

If the tables have turned, and you have been put in an uneasy situation by someone else, or the conversation is not going anywhere, and you find yourself locked in a dreaded silence, find an excuse to leave. If you are at a party, excuse yourself to get another drink, or tell the other person you need to say hello to a friend you have not gotten a chance to greet yet. At a networking function, simply thank them for your time. Make sure the other person knows you appreciate the time they took to speak with you, and if you have a reason for ending the conversation, clarify its validity to the other person.

As mentioned before, none of these tips are set in stone. Sometimes connections are made instantly, and the bonding can take effect quickly. The conversation can take a controversial turn that is not outside the comfort level of the participants and can continue without conflict. The best way to avoid unnecessary awkward moments is by truly taking the other person into consideration. Knowing that they are unique individuals, and have different responses to other people based on their personality and experiences. Observe and respect comfort levels, act and speak appropriately based on them, and use common sense.

Tips on Treating Social Anxiety Effectively

There are many problems in the world today that can cause people to feel awkward in social settings, from the standard fears of smelling bad to the extreme agoraphobia, and a lot of people fail to recognize the symptoms and underlying causes of these conditions. The most prevalent, and strangely the least treated, is social anxiety.

With the rise of technology people have become more and more accustomed to dealing with people through mediums, whether it is the phone or the internet, and this has caused a great many people to shy away from face to face interactions.

At first glance this may seem like technology has caused the problem, but the truth is that it has only enabled people who suffer from social anxiety to avoid most human interaction. If you are one of the many Americans who cannot help but feel terrified by the prospect of socializing then you need to explore ways of treating social anxiety in order to regain control of your life. The three tips below are designed to give you a general understanding of what to watch out for when you look for ways to find treatment:

1   The biggest problem people face when finding treatment is that they expect the best anxiety medication will completely

cure them of their problems, which makes them jump at the variety of advertisements that are shot out into the world like rock salt from a shotgun - meant to spray a wide area with something that is designed not to force your hand but simply alert you of its presence. That is how many of these companies are able to avoid large lawsuits for making false claims: they do not seek out people, but simply inform them of possible (if highly improbable) effects of their medication.

2   Although prescription medication can be highly effective the side effects are often far worse than the original problem. It is not worth trading chronic depression for explosive diarrhea and jitters. If you want to find something that will effectively treat your anxiety then you need to make sure it is 100% natural. By doing this you

can eliminate the possibilities of devastating side effects, while ensuring that you will have a product that will work with your body. Note: you still have to make sure that the products you get are not simple vitamins that parade around claiming to be anti anxiety medication because they will charge you an exorbitant amount of money for a product you could buy at the store for five dollars.

3 Once you are treating social anxiety with medications you have to commit yourself to improving your situation. By taking small, calculated risks - like going to a bar - you can create a mental space where you are capable of overcoming your rational fears. That way as the supplements take effect you are well-prepared to reclaim your place in society. You are half the treatment for your anxiety, and by coming

to understand that you will be able to improve your life dramatically.

CHAPTER 8

IMPROVE RELATIONSHIP WITH EMOTIONAL INTELLIGENCE

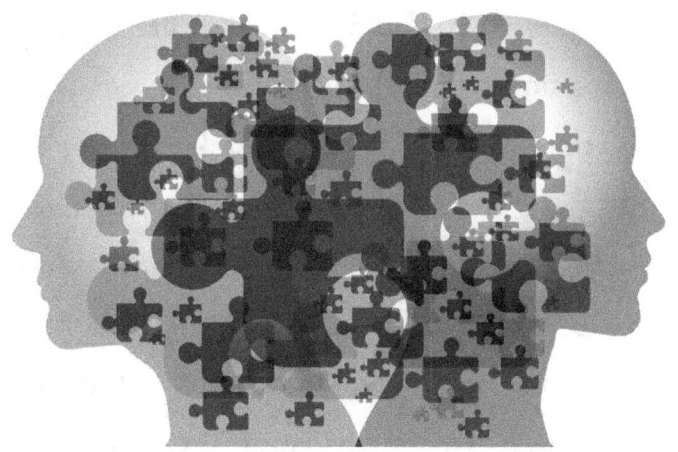

All of us intuitively know when we are about to have a difficult conversation or when a conversation becomes difficult, including when it is about to become difficult. Yet, there are very few of us who do not have difficult conversations almost every day of our life with our significant others, whether at work, at home or at play. Usually a difficult conversation means happens when we share (give and/or receive) negative feedback with anyone. That anyone may be a boss, spouse, good friend, child, colleague or someone we love and admire and care for. Some conversations can also seem difficult because we think that we have a lot at stake or we have already taken a position which we feel a retraction will lead to loss of face. Conversations also become difficult due to our past conditioning - we expect it to be difficult because it has been so in the past. We deal with conversations in a routine manner without stopping to reflect.

Reflection questions for a difficult conversation:

- Why do I want to have this conversation? (Self-awareness)

- What will happen by not having this conversation? What will happen by having this conversation? (Emotional maturity)

- What am I afraid of? What is the worst possible outcome? What is my stake? What do I expect - the best outcome? (Self-motivation)

- What untested assumptions and inferences am I making? How can I step into the space of the other person to test my assumptions and inferences so that I can understand all perspectives with equanimity? (Empathy and Understanding)

- Can I make a commitment to listen and understand and communicate that understanding? Can I just listen and not make any proposition until I have fully understood the other and have a confirmation to that effect? (Quality communication)

Social psychologists started looking at Emotional Intelligence in their studies of 'Social Intelligence'. E.L. Thorndike in 1920, was the first to identify Emotional Intelligence. We have moved away from IQ for intelligence to eleven kinds of intelligence. Psychologists have grouped them into three clusters:

- Abstract intelligence (the ability to understand and manipulate and apply verbal and mathematic symbols - the social and physical sciences).

- Concrete intelligence (the ability to understand and manipulate and with objects - engineering, construction, art).
- Social intelligence (interpersonal and intrapersonal relationships).

Thorndike defined social intelligence as, "The ability to understand and manage men and women, boys and girls - to act wisely in human relations." Gardner further improved upon this to include inter- and intrapersonal intelligences in his theory of multiple intelligences.

These two intelligences comprise social intelligence. He defines them as follows:

- Interpersonal intelligence is the ability to understand other people: what motivates them, how they work, how to work cooperatively with them. Successful salespeople, politicians, teachers, clinicians, and religious leaders are all likely to be individuals with high degrees of interpersonal intelligence.

- Intrapersonal intelligence is the ability to know and understand oneself accurately and truthfully and use that information effectively for inter-personal relationship as well as one's own personal growth and development..

Emotional Intelligence (often given the acronym EQ, the emotional-intelligence equivalent of IQ) is therefore knowing yourself and knowing others and integrating the two - balancing the head and the heart, combining the left and right brain, the ying and the yan, the masculine and the feminine. What we see, we see with our objective mind and then try to make meaning on the basis of our conditioning, life experiences and BS (Belief Systems). This coloring leads to an outcome from the subjective mind - therefore the perceiver perceives not what is perceived by the sensory organs but what the perceiver perceives as perceived with the help of the subjective mind. Based on this we either respond reactively or proactively - which we call within our control or not within our control.

For a long time IQ was considered the leading determinant of success - those who had a high IQ were expected to succeed. This however, was not always true. It is now proven that there are as many successful with a medium IQ score than high IQ score. There are even successful people with a low IQ score. Based on brain and behavioral research, Daniel Goleman argued that our IQ-oriented view of intelligence is far too limited and narrow as it ignores many other determinants of success. narrow. According to Goleman emotional intelligence (EQ) is the strongest indicator of human success. His definition of emotional intelligence includes self-awareness, emotional maturity, self-motivation, empathic understanding and quality communication. High EQ leads to higher success in work and relationships.

EQ can be developed through practice and learning. Most of us have forgotten to recognize our feelings. We often mistake our thinking for our feelings. Thus we have become far removed from ourselves.

EQ involves development of discriminatory knowledge - the difference between the perceiver and perceived, the subject and the object. To recognize others emotion and our own emotions as separate rather than mixing the two as a response to each other. There are five main abilities in EQ:

1. Self-awareness:

Knowing self. Being aware. Being aware of our physical, mental and emotional activities. To be in touch with ourselves. It takes practice to observe ourselves. Once we recognize our emotional state we can bring about changes to suit the situation.

2. Emotional maturity:

Once we are aware of our inner self, maturity means to face up to all the dimensions of ourselves without judgment. To accept things as they are. Having the courage to explore our blocks and to turn them around to help us to deal with our situations constructively.

3. Self-motivation:

Taking responsibility for our emotions and actions. Knowing that everything we do, we do for a reason and have a choice to do or not to do. When we make a choice, we do so to get away from pain and to receive pleasure. Pain and pleasure are the biggest two dimensions of motivation. Removal of pain moves us to great heights and then once we have removed pain we can move towards adding pleasure. This is our greatest motivation.

4. Empathic understanding:

Stepping out of one's own framework and entering the others mental model and looking at it entirely from the others point of view. To understand in the others framework and to communicate the understanding in the language of the other and to receive confirmation of that understanding, rather than adding any meaning of one's own to it.

5. Quality communication:

Active listening; communicating empathy and understanding; understanding before wanting to be understood.

EMPATHY ON RELATIONSHIP

Empathy allows us to form deeper more fulfilling emotional bonds with our loved ones. Empathy is the ability to feel and experience another's emotions, moods or attitude within our own body, as though it were our own feelings and sensations. It's much like compassion for another, only empathy takes understanding and compassion to a whole new level, giving you an actual physical experience in your own body. This is the ultimate act of love, mindfulness and complete surrender and can be very rewarding emotionally when you learn how to apply your innate empathic gifts to embrace the most important aspect of our lives, our personal connections with the ones you love.

Here are 5 easy steps to begin using empathy to enhance your relationships. Empathic relationships must be nurtured and understood in order to achieve the most from them.

1. Slow down and still your mind.

Your empathic sense is always available to you, but if you are distracted, you may not be receptive to its messages. Take a few moments each day to reflect on your relationships. Still your mind and focus on the positive things you are grateful for in your relationships. Concentrate on your loved ones special ⬚ualities and characteristics that bring you happiness. See your future relationship as having limitless potential, and opportunities for growth and understanding, making a solid connection impenetrable by any negative circumstance, event or obstacle.

2. Listen and Pay Attention

Empathy relies on the intelligence of the heart, teaches us mindfulness, and an understanding of the intricate connection we have to all living beings. Each time you respond to your intuitive empathic sense, you are reaching out to your loved ones and sending a message that you care. Listen carefully to what they are saying, even if you don't agree, this will create a strong foundation allowing your loved ones to feel safe in coming to you with their concerns, ideas or thoughts without fear or judgments. Listen with an open understanding heart, show interest in what is being said to you, and immerse yourself in the special moment of your loved one sharing of their thoughts and feelings with you.

3. Feel and Let go

Allow yourself to feel the emotions that come to you. Honor your feelings; even if you are feeling vulnerable, this will lead to strength and a deeper understanding of your experience. When you learn to understand and respect your own emotions, you will then be able to decipher your feelings from your loved ones. At times an empath will confuse others feelings for their own, and will quickly become overwhelmed. When you learn to separate these from one another, it will become clearer in how to find solutions for yourself and those around you. Once you have honored your feelings, release them and let them go. Feel proud that you have faced your feelings and have overcome difficulty and allow yourself to move on. This exercise will help you to learn to forgive and be forgiven.

Don't dwell on past issues, deal with them as they come, feel them and let them go.

4. Express yourself

The most important thing you can do as empath is to give love where it is needed, either to yourself or another person. When you begin to share your emotions, thoughts and ideas with others you clear the channels, sending a loving frequency, to those around you. Your relationships will begin to heal, creating deeper commitments and the focus will turn to healing in an environment conducive for a healthier relationship. Tell your partner, children, family and friends how much you love and appreciate them. They will respond to your loving energy, bringing you closer than ever.

5. Accept unconditionally

Accept yourself and your loved ones unconditionally. Learn to realize that our faults are part of who we are, but not necessarily the essence of our being. Acceptance is a form of expressing love, as we all need a place we can exist and be our true selves. Share this special gift, with your self and those you love.

Delve deeper into your own emotions, make it a point to personally take responsibility for your self and watch the relationships around you respond to your transformation, and your relationships will begin to grow and prosper and reach their true divine potential.

HOW TO USE EQ IN DIFFICULT CONVERSATIONS?

We can develop some general principles on how to have difficult conversations where EQ plays a very large role for the conversations to be win-win for both parties.

1. Clarify your own purpose and intent.

The EQ qualities of self-awareness and emotional maturity can help us to clarify our purpose and intent. Ask yourself why you wish to have this conversation? If your intention is unilateral - to have someone agree or support you - you are likely to have a very defensive response. If you really wish to move forward, you may enter the conversation with curiosity to explore the situation and verify the accuracy of your views. Knowing your own purpose and intent will help you to learn how to productively change your own behavior before having an impact on the other. Self-awareness helps you to clarify your intent and purpose.

Each difficult conversation is really about three things: what really happened, how you feel about what happened, and what the situation says about your identity. Get in touch with your thinking and feelings to know your fears and what your hot button issues are. This will help you to test your assumptions and attributions and validate your data. Some questions to test your emotional maturity:

- Am I being compassionate towards all?

- Am I open and curious or do I come with preconceived ideas? Am I willing to learn?

- Am I being transparent in sharing all I know?

- Am I fully committed to the outcome?

- What are my worst fears? What are my deepest desires?

- Am I holding myself accountable for my contributions?

2. Build a foundation for the conversation

Agree with the other person on the purpose of the conversation - what is it that you want to talk about? What is your interest in bringing about this conversation? Without this the other person is often more likely to stick with their own inferences and become defensive thereby not allowing you to make your proposition. Self-motivation is the quality that is most likely to help you as you know that you are having this conversation as a matter of choice - even though it is difficult. By using the qualities of empathy and understanding you can make the other person realize that this is not just a unilateral conversation but needs to be jointly discussed for mutual benefit. You can build the foundation in the four steps of:

- Don't just say what you think happened also ask for the others view of what they think happened.

- Talk about how the other feels and then share how you feel

- Proposition your interests after clarifying the others needs and interests

- Don't advocate solutions, ask for inputs to jointly design solutions

3. Stay focused on jointly designed process

Normally in difficult conversations we tend to go back to the history of the situation and lose track of the future goals as jointly designed. This will again require self-awareness and emotional maturity to be authentic, to realize where the process is getting derailed and to focus on the process. It will also require self-motivation to continue to the end of the process. Old data is often flawed as our reasoning is faulty when we are fearful of a situation or frustrated about a relationship. Self-motivated focus will help us to stay in the present and continue towards progress in the future.

4. Agree to monitor progress and discuss again

Success in difficult situations is achieved when both do something different. As this is about changing behaviour it is needed to fine-tune intentions with actions. Always agree to monitor progress and celebrate success at the end of difficult conversations.

It is indisputably true that each and every relationship is different and has a distinct, unique character; however, it is possible to distinguish three essential skills connected with emotional intelligence that play a significant role in relationship development. These skills are a crucial element required in establishing and improving relationships with others. The following article will provide you with some basic knowledge on what these skills are and how to use them in your everyday life.

STRESS MANAGEMENT

This skill is very important as stress seriously impedes your ability to feel, behave in a rational way, and to be emotionally available to others. To put it simply, it will disrupt any positive communication for as long as you and your partner feel insecure. With the feeling of safety comes the ability to pay proper attention to your partner. It's quite obvious that such situations damage the relationship. As a result, mastering the stress management skill will enable you to constantly maintain your emotional availability. The crucial stage in relationship help and improvement by means of emotional intelligence is the ability to perceive when the stress level is getting out of control. After you've properly assessed the danger you should channel your efforts to bringing yourself and others back to a comfortable and relaxed state of awareness.

EMOTION MANAGEMENT

The essential process of communication between you and your partner is maintained by means of emotional exchanges. These are usually triggered by basic emotions, such as sadness, anger, joy, fear or disgust. If you want to communicate with the intention of focusing someone's attention and making them involved in the exchange, you must gain access to your core emotions and then evaluate how your actions and relationship are affected by them.

You must also bear in mind that your emotions might be, sometimes very easily, distorted, numbed, or buried. People are especially susceptible to this after they experienced some kind of trauma, for example isolation, loss or abuse. Sadly, it is impossible to fully embrace one's motivation and life needs without inducing at least some emotional awareness. Therefore, lack of such awareness will also damage the ability to effectively communicate with others. Proper recognition of one's core emotions is a key element of staying emotionally healthy and emotionally intelligent.

CHAPTER 9

<u>ENHANCE EMPATHY</u>

Empathy is really important because it helps us connect you with other people and with their feelings and emotions. Empathy helps you to bond with your child, with your partner, with your close friends, and with other people that you care about. Empathy can also help you out when you have to deal with a difficult person.

People can develop empathy and if you believe that you have mediocre or poor skills in this area, you should know that you can improve them.

First of all we should understand what empathy is and how we could define it. Empathy is when you put yourself in someone else' s shoes, when you really understand his problems: empathy helps us get closer to another person and it helps us gain that person' s trust.

Usually, when we empathize with someone, we enhance and strengthen the relationship and we are making it closer. Sometimes, empathy is often the beginning of an interaction because it means that you not only know what the person is going through, but you are also concerned about her ongoing mood. This shows that you are not a self-centered person as well.

Nowadays people are too busy and self-absorbed and they forget to pay attention to people around them. They do not the time or the energy to deal with other people's problems. It is difficult to care about others when you have your own issues, but still, we should not forget that we are human beings and that we should help each other as much as we can.

Empathy is an essential part of emotions and is itself a specific emotion involving a feeling element of connection and a bodily reaction of verbal or non verbal communication. Empathy in general would mean feeling what the other person is feeling and 'being in the shoes of the other'. Empathy creates emotional link and involvement and could be between lovers, family members, friends, or even strangers. Empathy relates to connectedness and a sense of just knowing what another person is feeling. Some individuals are simply more empathetic than others whereas some individuals could find it hard to relate. Some questions that psychology would deal with are what creates empathy and why are some individuals more empathetic than others.

Empathy or a feeling of connectedness and being in the shoes of others, is closely related to intuition as intuition helps in the understanding and recognition of emotions in others. Even if emotions are covert and not manifested, empathy helps in identifying these emotions through intuition. Empathy is thus described as recognizing other people's emotions through intuition and is marked by a feeling of connecting to the other person.

In any leadership situation such as in political leadership and social leadership, it is necessary for leaders to feel certain degree of empathy with the other members of the group as the leaders have to feel connected to the followers to make an impact in their opinions and decisions. Teachers also have to feel empathy with the students as this creates a connectedness without which the teaching experience is meaningless both for the teachers and the students. Empathy is about motivating or influencing the other person by tapping in on his or her emotions. It is easier to influence or change people if you are keenly aware of what they are thinking or feeling as this helps to predict the possible responses. Finally we have understanding of other people only when we are able to predict their responses and empathy adds a predictive quality to the interaction.

STAGES OF EMPATHY

It could be said that empathy begins with intuition and ends with prediction is which one person is able to predict the emotional responses of the other. The stages of empathy are thus given as:

- Intuition
- Connection
- Consideration
- Prediction
- Motivation

The first stage of intuition involves one person naturally intuitive towards the other as with intuition of the other person's emotions and feelings or thought processes, the next stage of empathy or a feeling of connectedness is established. The connection between two people naturally leads to a feeling of mutual consideration and the next stage of predicting each other's responses. In some cases empathy could be mutual although in many cases as in a relationship between a therapist and her patient, the empathy could be one sided. After the connection is established and there is a deep sense of consideration for the other's feelings, and an understanding as to why the person is feeling in a particular way, one person who empathizes with the other is able to move to the next stage of predicting the emotional responses. Understanding the response patterns in other people is an essential part of connecting and relating to them closely and would definitely suggest the ability of being in the shoes of the other. The last stage of empathy deals with the more directional aspect as in the case of teacher or therapist there is a need to motivate or influence the other person following an empathetic connection. In fact the empathy may have been established to influence the other person to attain some goals or reach some targets. So influencing and motivating the other person is an integral part of empathy and is a tacit goal of empathetic relations.

Apart from the five stages of empathy discussed, empathy could involve subsequent feelings of friendship, love, rapport, admiration, dependence and this would depend on whether the empathy is between a teacher and a student, a therapist and a patient, a leader and his followers or between lovers or friends.

From a psychological point of view, empathy would involve fulfilling the safety and security needs of other individuals and also their love and belongingness needs. Empathy needs are thus somewhere in between the love-attachment-belongingness (psychological) needs of individuals and the safety-security needs of individuals and the need for empathy exists in every individual and is manifested in both the forms of giving and receiving empathy.

Individuals fulfil their love and belongingness needs by relating to others and empathy uses love and belongingness to provide safety and security. Thus the purpose of empathy as explained with Maslow's hierarchy of needs theory is to make the other person happy by providing a sense of security and lending support as is the goal of empathy could mean a positive influence of one person on the other. Empathy highly enhances social interaction as it adds elements of familiarity, connectedness and consideration between people and help to instill and maintain human values.

THEORY AND THERAPY

Apart from the Maslow's basic needs theory which would identify empathy as a love and safety need, any psychotherapeutic framework could successfully utilize the concept of empathy and develop a therapeutic model based on affective interaction between therapist and client. In fact any client centred therapy requires empathetic connection between the client and the therapist and development of an Affective Therapeutic System based on the Intuition-Connection-Consideration-Prediction-Motivation (ICCPM) model of empathy could be an effective method of therapy in which different stages of empathy are identified and evoked between the client and the therapist to reach the final goal of mutual understanding.

For example if a client suffers from depression, the Affective Therapeutic Framework can use the

ICCPM model to first emphasize on developing intuitive interaction between the client and the therapist. This is possible after a background or history of the client's illness or psychological condition is obtained by the therapist. The intuitive stage in which the client and therapist develops a subconscious bond is followed by a sense of connectedness when the client begins to open up to the therapist and communication becomes easy. The third stage of consideration follows as both client and therapist decide to cooperate on a specific goal and begins to understand each other's language. The fourth stage of therapeutic interaction would be based on both the client and therapist being able to predict reactions and responses and empathetically connect to each other's opinions. The last stage of therapy deals with decision making and evaluation to see whether the motivational levels of the client have been improved and whether the therapist has been an influential factor in changing the behaviour or thought process of the client.

One of the easiest and earliest signs/omens to observe and recognize, and identify the potential of a specific individual, to do what's in the best interests of his organization, and its stakeholders, is whether he spends more time listening intently and thoroughly to others, or merely dominating conversations by speaking more than he listens! Beware of the difference between someone who merely claims to care about his constituents, and the ideal individual, who effectively listens to others (both those he agrees with/supporters, as well as those that disagree/opponents). Because this difference is often less than easily obvious, it is easy to confuse zealous rhetoric, with really caring. Those hoping to become great leaders, who make an important difference, must consistently proceed with genuine EMPATHY.

1   Energetic; earn respect; expectations: How can anyone know that your intents are pure and well-meaning, until and unless, you proceed with constant and motivating energy? People hope to gain energy from their leaders! This is a first, essential step, in the process of earning respect, and attracting others to become more involved and motivate! While your goals must be far-reaching and important, it is important to manage expectations of others, so as to avoid disappointments! Do this, however, in a way, where you under-promise, and over-deliver!

2   Make most; mind; matters: Always make the most of your potential, and your skills and ability, by proceeding in an organized, well-prepared manner. Groucho Marx is credited with saying, "It's a matter of mind over matter. If you don't have a mind, it doesn't matter."

Leading is not about merely possessing knowledge, but rather transforming gathering facts, to effective, proactive action. Know what matters, and do what's needed, to best serve the needs and priorities of your constituents.

3   Pleasantries; positions; priorities: A great leader does not mean to be the most sociable person in the room, but must be considered approachable and pleasant, so others feel comfortable and confident, speaking to him, and providing better insight into their needs and priorities. Take a position, and make it clear and in accordance with your objectives, and focus on serving others. Proceed with a priority-based perspective, and proactively proceed forward, continuously.

4   Attitude; alternatives: Some people ascend to a leadership position, and falsely

believe, it means they are able to proceed with the My way, or the highway, approach. However, a genuine leader, subordinates his ego and personal agenda, and prioritizes the best interests of others. Proceeding with a true, positive attitude, combined with an open-mind and a willingness to review, and consider alternatives, enhances one's ability to empathize.

5 Timely; together: Never procrastinate, but once you've carefully reviewed and evaluated, and ask pertinent and relevant questions, proceed with timely action. The goal must be to continuously demonstrate that we are all in this together!

6 Healing; head/heart; humane: Empathetic leaders heal wounds, and seek a meeting of the minds, and an open discussion of differences, in a solution-seeking approach. Avoid either an overly

emotional, or logical approach, but realize that a combination of one;s emotions and logic, in a head/heart balance, is the best way to create a true connection! Never forget that a leader must consider people, and always be humane, with your actions, as well as your words/rhetoric.

7   Yes: Don't be so rigid that you are afraid to say yes to possibilities, and consider alternatives and options.

How can anyone lead without being empathetic? True leaders always focus on genuine EMPATHY!

There is often a significant difference between having sympathy for someone, and feeling empathy. In most cases, sympathy includes feeling sorry for someone, while empathy is when we put ourselves in someone else's place, and feel and appreciate what they are going through and feeling. Often, empathy is far more difficult because it re⬚uires a genuine act of caring, and taking action, while sympathy is often little more than a polite form of lip service. In leadership situations, this difference becomes far more essential, because it means making a concerted effort to understand and appreciate other viewpoints and ponts of view, which may at times be in conflict with the leader's personal position. However, true leaders realize that in order to provide true value and make an organization relevant, a leader must understand what others want, need, and desire, and why.

1   The empathic leader reaches out to others, especially in difficult and trying times. Empathy is far more, however, than simply feeling one's pain, but rather getting to understand its cause and effects. One of the greatest challenges facing today's leaders is making their organization maintain its relevance, and

enhancing its sustainability. The only way an organization can do this over a significant period of time is to continuously evolve. Only when leaders can relate to their constituents, and understand that what the rank and file is searching for is often quite different from what those in leadership are considering. How can any leader make his group relevant if he does not empathize with the desires and needs of others.

2   One of the most often repeated leadership errors is to say they are sorry, or to feel sorry for others. Most human beings tend to resent when those we don't know personally and often closely, show sympathy and appear to be feeling sorry for them. People want to be understood and cared for, and most importantly, have their viewpoints considered and understood. Only when leaders are

empathic can they fully relate to, and understand, what their constituents are askinwoofer, and even more importantly, are considering, most important and relevant. Great leadership can generally be measured by how well a leader listens and understands, and how his actions reflect the needs of others. True leaders always provide quality and value!

Do the leaders you know really want to know and understand what you think and want, or do they sis,ply go through the motions? Only empathic leaders ever truly relate to their constituents.

CHAPTER 10

<u>DOES YOUR BRAND HAVE</u>
<u>EMOTIONAL INTELLIGENCE?</u>

A lot of research has been done in the field of EQ for many years. It's only more recently been brought to the forefront by leading experts-to name a few: Daniel Goleman in Working with Emotional Intelligence, Robert E. Kelley in How to Be a Star at Work and Travis Bradberry and

Jean Greaves in The Emotional Intelligence Quick Book.

So, what is Emotional Intelligence anyway? According to Daniel Goleman it is "the capacity for recognizing our own feelings and those of others, for motivating ourselves, for managing emotions well in ourselves and in our relationships."

EQ alone explains 58% of a leader's job performance (TalentSmart®). 90% of top performers are high in EQ (TalentSmart®). A study of 200 companies worldwide indicates a difference in productivity (Goleman) - 1/3 of the difference is due to technical skill and cognitive ability - while 2/3 is due to emotional competence.

Have you ever experienced a situation as a customer with an employee (of the company you were doing business with) who was just totally unaware? The employee didn't and couldn't even recognize their own emotions as they were occurring? You could see it in their face and body language. And as they couldn't acknowledge their emotions they experienced within themselves, it was impossible for them to manage their emotions as they interacted with you; let alone aware of the subtle or overt cues from you so they could respond in a positive and productive way to your needs.

These types of situations are further intensified when you experience the same thing over and over with a company with whom you are doing business, until finally you say "ENOUGH! I can't take it anymore!" Well, think about this. The majority of customers (and I bet you're one of them) WANT TO DO BUSINESS with the brands you frequent; but companies and their employees just give you REASONS NOT to!

Take the airline industry for example. If more airlines focused on hiring and developing their people for emotional intelligence, they would be a lot more productive and have a lot more satisfied customers. One of my recent experiences involved a flight cancellation. It was due to a mechanical issue and lack of availability of a replacement aircraft and alternate airline flight to my destination city. Although disappointed, all my fellow passengers were eager to get rebooked as we stampeded like a herd of cattle to the gate agent desk.

As I was standing in line, I overheard one of the gate agents say that our luggage was being forwarded to the destination city anyway. I looked at another passenger. We raised our eyebrows in unison. We were commanded to stay behind without our luggage. No "say-so" in the matter. A lot of customers scheduled for this flight didn't even live in this city (including

'MOI'). The thought of our luggage being sent in advance was absurd! As you can imagine, we all began to question the logic. Someone asked, "How can you ship our luggage if you don't have a plane to fly?" Obviously, it made no sense whatsoever.

The situation brewed like a magical potion in the pot. The 'herd' grumbled and expressed further displeasure with comments like, "That's B___ S___! "You can't possibly be serious!" and so forth. It became very apparent that this gate agent was irritated with our complaints as she suddenly yelled out, "I don't appreciate your tone with me. I expect to be treated with respect!" She was so absorbed in her own emotions that she could no longer recognize her lack of self-awareness and put herself in our multitude of shoes; let alone manage the situation productively.

My fellow passengers fumed as this gate agent refused to question the original information received about our luggage. We pleaded with her to reconfirm. Needless to say, we were outraged with her behavior and lack of sensitivity. The gate agent next her was very aware and tried to smooth things over. It was he who picked up the phone for clarification on the luggage situation and after further investigation...he gently whispered in her ear, we received inaccurate information. He then proceeded to inform us our luggage would be at baggage claim so and so. Oh, I must say, his colleague was not pleased. She was so self-absorbed and unaware of her emotions and actions. She just huffed!

When I look back on this situation-it is so amusing to me now. A lot of goodwill was lost to customers doing business with this airline because of this one employee's lack of emotional intelligence. Multiply this every time it is experienced again and again with the same company and their employees who lack the basic skills of emotional intelligence, which by the way can be learned. Yes EQ is a learnable skill. We can train the brain, unlike IQ (our capacity to learn) and personality, which form around the age of 5 and remain virtually unchanged over the course of our life.

So, that brings us to the question, what is Brand Emotional Intelligence? Brand Emotional Intelligence (EQ) is the extent, to which your business acknowledges, understands and manages your employees and customers so as to enhance the perceived value of your brand. The concept of Brand EQ was derived by The Brand Ascension Group LLC based on the extensive research by Daniel Goleman on Emotional Intelligence which demonstrates there is more to an individual's success than just being "smart." Emotional Intelligence is an intangible part of each of us that tunes into personal and social nuances about emotions, and when used effectively can drive actions and decisions that deliver positive results. It is a significant part of personal and professional success for people at all levels in business. Unlike IQ, EQ can be learned, developed and improved over time.

The same concept of individual emotional intelligence holds true for the collective emotions within your organization and how they affect your customers impacting their emotions and perceptions created as a result of their experience with your brand (your employees). Your customers (who are human beings) constantly perceive information. They take in thousands of bits of information through all their senses: sight, sound, taste, touch, smell and intuition. They process this information, form opinions and judgments, and make decisions based on this data. Being fully conscious of the knowledge of how your customers' constantly perceive your brand can better enable you to consistently create positively, memorable experiences for them.

Brand Emotional Intelligence is made up of four distinct dimensions that cover how organizations recognize and manage behaviors both internally and externally to drive the desired customer perception:

Internal Brand Emotional Awareness - is your organization's ability to accurately perceive the varied and collective emotions, behaviors and perceptions of your employees and how these drive customer perceptions. Do you stay abreast of how your employees tend to respond to specific situations and people, and how these positively or negatively impact the Brand Promise?

Internal Brand Relationship Management - is your organization's ability to use awareness of the collective emotions, behaviors and perceptions, and harness the hearts and minds of your employees to positively direct their behavior. Do you manage employees effectively to drive the "desired culture," reinforcing the behaviors that deliver on your Brand Promise?

External Brand Emotional Awareness - is your organization's ability to readily recognize and assess the emotions and behaviors of customers, understanding what drives customer perception; and what customers are thinking and feeling and anticipating their wants and desires. Do you investigate what drives customers' opinions and judgments about your brand to understand their perception and if it is congruent with your Brand Promise?

External Brand Relationship Management - is your organization's ability to use the awareness and assessment of the emotions of your customers to internally and externally manage, direct and adapt quickly to drive increases in positive customer perceptions. Do you stay on top of what it takes to create positively, memorable customer experiences congruent with your Brand Promise to create increased brand equity and perceived value? If you answered no to any of the questions, then your organization has missed some key opportunities to build Brand Emotional Intelligence.

If You have a few moments, I would appreciate a review on Amazon, if You found your new book useful in any way.

Enjoy !

PS: sure the target is correct, take a look at my other published book, You should like it ->

" HOW TO ANALYZE PEOPLE:

5 minutes for read body language, analyze personality type and better your relationship. Learn the secrets to human psychology, step by step. "